Beatrix Campbell is a print and broadcasting journalist. She worked for ten years on the *Morning Star* and was a founder member of the Women's Liberation journal *Red Rag*. From 1979 she was a reporter with *Time Out*. Together with the majority of the staff she left after a long occupation and strike to defend equal pay for all and workers' right to consultation and set up the co-operatively owned magazine *City Limits*, where she worked as a reporter until 1988. With Anna Coote she co-authored the best-selling book *Sweet Freedom*. Virago published *Wigan Pier Revisited*, her rendezvous with George Orwell's classic and which was the winner of the 1984 Cheltenham Festival prize for Literature. In 1987 her book *The Iron Ladies* was the winner of the Fawcett Prize, followed by *Unofficial Secrets: The Cleveland Case* in 1988. In 1989 she was awarded the 300 Committee's Nancy Astor Campaigning Journalist of the Year. In 1990 Channel 4 broadcast her award-winning documentary on the Nottingham ritual abuse case, which was followed by *Goliath: Britain's Dangerous Places*, her book on the 1991 riots in Britain. She is visiting professor of Women's Studies at the University of Newcastle-upon-Tyne.

Also by Beatrix Campbell

Sweet Freedom
Wigan Pier Revisited
The Iron Ladies: Why Do Women Vote Tory?
Goliath: Britain's Dangerous Places

unofficial
secrets

child sexual abuse:
the cleveland case

Beatrix Campbell

A *Virago* book

Published by Virago Press 1988

Reprinted 1989, revised edition 1997

A CIP catalogue record for this book is available from the British
Library

ISBN 1 86049 284 3

Typeset by M Rules in Plantin
Printed and bound in Great Britain by
Clays Ltd, St Ives plc

Virago
A Division of
Little, Brown and Company (UK)
Brettenham House
Lancaster Place
London WC2E 7EN

CONTENTS

ACKNOWLEDGEMENTS

Since the first edition of *Unofficial Secrets* my thinking about Cleveland and its consequences has developed in encounters with groups of professionals and survivors of sexual crime. The Cleveland report set the scene for the theft histories which were re-interpreted and recruited for a crusade against survivors and those professionals who tried to protect them. They, like the Cleveland professionals before them, didn't deserve what was to come.

INTRODUCTION

One morning early in the summer of 1987 a story appeared on the front page of a national newspaper which didn't make sense. The story ran and ran, measuring more column inches than any other single saga that year – and yet the story went on not making sense. Nevertheless, it became a defining moment in the British state's response to childhood adversity.

This was the Cleveland case, the story of 121 'innocent' children being snatched from their 'innocent' parents by practitioners perceived as witchdoctors so suspicious of sexual abuse that they saw signs of it everywhere – including in children's bottoms. 'Innocence' itself became an actor in this drama, an impersonator, disturbing the safe categories of victim and culprit which had shaped the statutory services in the image of Freudian fantasy: after all, sex doesn't happen to children – unless they incite it. And sex doesn't happen in bottoms. Unless you're queer.

These fundamental principles of sexual ideology were confounded in the Cleveland case: the ghost of budding Lolitas inciting incontinent men was undermined by the average age of the Cleveland cohort: six. And the orthodoxy of the orifice was shaken by the evidence that a baby in a buggy, with a very sore bottom, was being buggered by her father.

The Cleveland case challenged our world view about sex. It also became a crisis of knowing, of what is known and how it may become knowable. As the months and then the years went by, we were not allowed to know what had happened in Cleveland.

Just as there was a determined not-knowing in 1987, there was equal resistance to any attempt to follow up those 121 children, and a reluctance to co-ordinate re-referrals. Some children did return to the attention of the statutory services. Some children did go on enduring abuse by adults who – having been acquitted by the public debate – had permission to carry on.

Despite being reassured by its own Social Services Inspectorate that the Cleveland health and welfare professionals were behaving professionally, the government suddenly that summer announced a judicial inquiry, not into the phenomenon but into the response to it. Its brief led to another episode in the crisis of knowing. The inquiry conspicuously evaded the questions on everyone's lips: 'What has happened to these children? What brought them to the attention of the statutory services? What do the signs scripted across their bodies mean?'

The government guaranteed that these questions would not be asked or answered. In cases of alleged sexual abuse there has always been something more important than knowing – and that is not knowing. Government ministers interpreted the many clues peppering the Cleveland report as if nothing had happened to the children. The judicial inquiry was itself muted, both by its brief and by the fate of cases coming before the civil courts and being routinely thrown out because, whatever the evidence, they were controversial.

Of course they were. But reviewing the crisis after nearly a decade I am abashed at what we thought was controversial.

For example, the first edition of this book contains an interview with a man and a woman whose children all showed worrying symptoms. The father was already a convicted sex offender. He was candid: yes, he had 'previous'; he confessed and then retracted. His explanation for anal and vaginal medical signs? He didn't have one. I didn't believe his protestations, but I faithfully reported his story. And I didn't ask why his career as a sex offender and his absurd alibis weren't relevant.

If this case was controversial, it was not because a convicted sex offender was given custody of his children. It was because Dr Marietta Higgs' diagnosis had ignited an investigation. If this case was controversial, it was not because the convicted sex offender made a confession – like his previous record, that didn't matter. It was as if Dr Higgs, not the man with convictions and a confession, had to be found guilty. Revisiting his case has been a revelation: what would now be interpreted as significant – convictions and a confession – were then irrelevant; they were put to one side and made to not matter. Since then, he has been the subject of a new investigation – based, this time, not on signs but on a story of sexual abuse.

During 1987 the civil courts were pre-empting the outcome of the judicial inquiry by throwing out many of the local authority's applications. The judge, Elizabeth Butler-Sloss, might have wished that Cleveland County Council had pressed its case more combatively because the inquiry's report did not criticise the dismissal of these applications.

So, although the government acted as though nothing had happened, it read the Cleveland report knowing that *something* had indeed happened to many, if not most, of the children. Its own inspectorate should have already known this, as should the medical and legal establishment.

What did they know? That the signs scrolled on the bodies of children suggested serious sexual abuse – the Cleveland report said so. They also knew that, if the children had indeed been abused, then the signs were telling us something more – that the children were so marooned in their abusers' needs and pressure and point of view that silence was itself a survival strategy. A tactic of accommodation was revealed by the signs: the architecture of the body suggested the anatomy of adaptation, of small bodies adapting to overwhelming intrusion, orifices scarred and altered by incoming objects, orifices speaking into the silence of their young subjects.

Not all the children were silent. Some spoke loudly and clearly. Some spoke obliquely and hesitantly. But the adult community chose to interpret the silence – rather than the signs – as the relief of suspicion, rather than as a clue to the difficulty of disclosure. Instead of interpreting the matrix of signs and silence as a dynamic, as a drama of physical suffering and survival shrouded by secrecy, it chose an interpretation of this eerie scenario that reinstated the ideologies and institutions that were so stiffly challenged by these children.

Thereafter, a determination to act as if it did not know what had happened to the Cleveland children defined the disposition of the government. The 'top men', the medical and legal establishment gossiped over cocktails and confided to each other that well, yes, those doctors probably got it right. Reports were written and sent to ministers and then never revealed to you and me.

When the judicial panel inquired into the response by

professionals it never investigated the range of responses by perpetrators – the absent presence in the whole debate. Experts who worked with perpetrators were shunned. The only evidence the inquiry heard about alleged abusers came from an American advocate for the accused, Ralph Underwager, an itinerant 'expert witness' who specialised in giving evidence on behalf of defendants, whose confidence in the campaign to discredit children's evidence of abuse prompted him to pronounce only five years later that paedophiles should proudly proclaim their sexual desire for children as the will of God.

The government and the inquiry report never asked or answered the question: What do we do to protect endangered children when the children themselves do not, or cannot, protest? Just as silence as a strategy, as a source of agency amid calamities that did not originate with the child, was not assimilated, neither was the weight of children's fear, nor their dissociation as another survival strategy to protect themselves from chronic, extreme pain. Far from learning from the children's difficulties, the government's procedures actually relied upon them, regulating even more intensely the limits upon the space and time available to children to begin to speak. That is the scandal of Cleveland.

The irony is that in 1987 the Department of Health was already well aware of all this and more. When it set up the judicial inquiry, the Department, social services staff and the police were themselves already addressing a different difficulty: how to help children who had a complaint to make. All over the country statutory services were struggling with the same things: how to help children who were speaking, protesting, to get justice; how to listen, gather evidence, consolidate a case, and protect children in danger; how to help doctors become definite instead of defensive; how to help the child psychiatric services embrace the possibility of an external event.

The typical difficulty for child protection workers was the absence of medical signs to corroborate strong stories that rarely survived the rough journey to the criminal courts. Here were physical signs that had been regarded as forensic gold. If the revelation of Cleveland was the closed circuit of strong signs and silence (although we must never forget that some of the Cleveland children did speak), then the inquiry's shift from the signs to the silence was an intimation of collusive cynicism – once the argument about the signs was settled, the inquiry turned its mind not to the question of silence, but to how to patrol the possibility that children might speak.

Bizarrely, the protocols written in the aftermath of the Cleveland inquiry prescribed procedures which, according to one child protection specialist, were designed to police the professionals and to control the conditions in which children might speak. They were propelled not by the interests of children trying to tell their story, nor by those of children whose bodies might be signifying acts that had silenced them, but by the regulation of conflict created by children's evidence, both between adults and children and between professionals.

Those with an investment in silence, accused adults – sometimes called parents – appeared as the victims of a new contagion: system abuse. And the arrangements created in the aftermath gave even convicted sex offenders the right to participate in planning the futures of the very children they had oppressed. 'The fact that they were parents was more important than anything,' said the specialist. 'When I saw the list of participants at a case conference and read that minutes were to be sent to the father in prison, and that the Governor was to be approached to invite him to the next meeting, I knew it was all finished, particularly for his children who were terrified every night they went to bed that he'd come and get them again. Of course, they were right. The procedures ensured that he would.' That is the codicil to Cleveland's bequest to British children.

The first edition of this book was written during the Cleveland controversy. At the time, journalists' access to the professional protagonists was rendered virtually impossible by the strictures of the inquiry itself and by a proper respect for its interrogations. Like everyone else, including the protagonists, I imagined that the Cleveland inquiry was serious about seeking the truth. But we were all thinking in a mindset framed by the focus of the inquiry. Like many other observers, I was drawn into a debate in which the participants were never allowed to know what was knowable, and in which anger was directed not at alleged abusers but at children's advocates.

Now, I wonder why. And I wonder why, like most other people, I reserved my restless discomfort for the people who had decided to do something about the evidence before their eyes. That disposition did not mute a critique of the outrageous mutiny by the police, the most masculinised public service, who seemed to abandon their duty to investigate and to co-operate with their colleagues. They were the detonators, but their behaviour never aroused anger. Was that because Britain was already pessimistic about the police, the one agency that cannot be called to account? The report's criticisms of the police didn't matter: no one noticed; no one was disciplined. But, nevertheless, that discomfort still lies like permafrost across the enduring controversies about child abuse. We still think nothing happened. We're still angry with the wrong people.

Lateral thinking was the only thing that could help make sense of the story of the signs and silences at the crux of this case. So I talked to child protection professionals and members of survivors' movements elsewhere in Britain and in Ireland. They weren't surprised by the signs – they'd already encountered them. They weren't surprised by the combustion, either, because professional conflicts and political panic were endemic to sexual crime, not least because it obliged services to identify with history's culprits: women and children. Cleveland could have been anywhere.

Now I understand the meaning of the meeting which begins this book's narrative. It was initiated by child protection workers in Nottingham, West Yorkshire and the West Midlands who were trying to tell politicians that the scale and seriousness of the problem were straining their resources, too. They were also asking: 'What are we supposed to do about this?' Why weren't people like this invited to the inquiry?

When Elizabeth Butler-Sloss reported that she had no reason to doubt the medical findings in Cleveland, professionals and the public could reasonably infer that the doctors might have been right. But that would have been wrong, because the message inferred by some from that report was that it didn't matter. Those doctors had – with the arrogance of innocence – blown the whistle. They thought their suspicions of secretive and successful abuse that imperilled the well-being of their patients might have mattered.

They were wrong. What mattered more was that the sovereignty of services built on an acceptable level of abuse was retrieved and their reputation restored. I did not understand that at the time.

Confidential documents written by the regional health

authorities after they had digested the Cleveland report are exclusively revealed in this new edition. They confirm what was only coded at the time: that the government and the health authorities had reason to believe that the doctors were probably right, but that no one would know. That is the scandal of Cleveland.

CHRONOLOGY OF EVENTS

1983   Judicial policy on sexual crimes is challenged in the wake of national scandals about the treatment of women reporting rape.

A television documentary on Thames Valley detectives' treatment of a woman reporting a rape shocks the nation. The Home Office responds by recommending that women should be able to request examinations by women officers and doctors.

Tyneside Women Police Doctors Group is set up on the initiative of Northumbria Police and Tyneside Rape Crisis Centre. It is immediately deluged not with adult rape survivors but with sexually abused children.

Leeds paediatricians, psychologists and social workers take up child sex abuse.

Dr Geoffrey Wyatt appointed consultant paediatrician at Middlesbrough General Hospital.

1984   The Metropolitan Police, dissatisfied with traditional methods, sets up a working party to review methods of interviewing children alleged to have been sexually assaulted. The Met's working party recommends joint investigation of child sexual abuse in the family between the police and social services. The London borough of Bexley is selected by the Met for a pilot study of co-operative methods, which becomes the model of good practice.

1985   Republic of Ireland sets up a national sexual assault treatment unit, the result of co-operation between the police and women doctors in Dublin for the treatment of rape survivors. It is immediately besieged with child sexual abuse cases.

Cleveland's Area Review Committee, a forum to co-ordinate child protection agencies' work on child abuse, sets up a working party, chaired by the NSPCC, to design new systems for dealing with sexual abuse. After several months the police management reject its proposals for joint investigations.

1986   Leeds paediatricians Jane Wynne and Christopher Hobbs publish in the *Lancet* their pioneering study of buggery as a common sign of child sexual abuse. Their diagnosis, anal dilatation, is fiercely criticised by Manchester police surgeon, Raine Roberts. Their work remains, however, the only statistical breakdown of buggery among children referred to hospital doctors, and is confirmed by the experience of the doctors working with sexually abused children in Tyneside and Dublin.

Cleveland constabulary management reject a working party compromise on joint interviews.

Cleveland County Council declares child abuse a priority and appoints a special consultant, Sue Richardson, to plan its programme of work. Sue Richardson criticises Cleveland Constabulary for failing to attend child abuse case conferences.

1987

Jan   Dr Marietta Higgs is appointed consultant paediatrician at Middlesbrough General Hospital.
Total Cleveland child sexual abuse cases, 25.

Feb   A new joint child abuse committee replaces the
Area Review Committee working party, and history repeats itself with the same arguments over
police primacy and autonomy in investigations.
    Dr Higgs is called in to give a second opinion
after a police surgeon refers a case of suspected
sexual abuse to social services. Total sexual abuse
cases, 33. Dr Higgs diagnoses anal dilatation.

March   Parents begin to dispute the anal dilatation diagnosis being reached by Middlesbrough General
Hospital. Total sexual abuse cases, 30.

April   The number of sexual abuse cases being diagnosed by the hospital increases, pushing up the
total tally to 43.

May   The police management rejects joint investigations. The total sexual abuse cases almost doubles
to 81. The police treat uncorroborated diagnoses
of sexual abuse with scepticism. Relations
between police and social services break down.

June   Sexual abuse referrals by the hospital peak. Total
sexual abuse cases, 110. The police withdraw
from investigations and break off relations with
social services. Social services speedily set up a
special Children's Resource Centre at the hospital. Parents in argument in Ward 9. Nurses

distressed. Police are called. Paediatricians asked by management to reduce the number of sexual abuse admissions. They refuse. Paediatricians are later advised that they are not being instructed to reduce admissions, but are warned about concern among district hospital management.

Social services director Mike Bishop agrees to arrangements for a second-opinion panel to be set up, to which parents may send their children. Stuart Bell, MP for Middlesbrough, objects to the presence on the panel of Leeds paediatrician Jane Wynne.

Bell accuses Sue Richardson and Marietta Higgs, in a Parliamentary speech, of 'colluding and conspiring' to keep the police out of sexual abuse investigations. Parents visiting their children in the hospital's Ward 9 rebel. The Rev Michael Wright helps organise Parents' Support Group. The Community Health Council helps dissenting parents contact the support group. Police surgeon Dr Alistair Irvine criticises anal dilatation diagnosis in public. Cleveland constabulary issues press statement accusing Sue Richardson of replacing old arrangements with new guidelines. A round robin among hospital staff supporting the paediatricians sent to management.

July   Stuart Bell writes to the government's Health Minister, Tony Newton, alleging that Cleveland Social Services are empire-building and accuses two councillors of being 'put up' by social services to recommend an extension of the department's role in the field of child abuse. Bell sends the minister his 'dossier' on parents.

13

Drs Higgs and Wyatt on leave from the hospital. Total child abuse cases down to 39. After perusing Stuart Bell's dossier on the Cleveland cases, Tony Newton announces the judicial inquiry into Cleveland in the wake of public disquiet.

August Finally, the police concede joint investigations.

October Mrs Justice – later Lord and then Dame – Elizabeth Butler-Sloss presides over the judicial inquiry in Middlesbrough Town Hall until the end of the year. The paediatricians, parents, police, county council, health authorities and the local government officers' association – the social service staff union – are all represented. There are widespread predictions in the press that the inquiry will discredit the diagnosis.

Suspected sexual abuse referrals by the hospital cease.

1988 Cleveland report published.
Dec Drs Higgs and Wyatt banned from sexual abuse work.

1989
Feb Three hundred people attend community meeting organised by members of the local government union NUPE (now Unison) and the Communist Party. The meeting launches campaign against child abuse, CAUSE, which conducts house-to-house surveys and conferences bringing experts to the county. Labour-controlled county council hostile to CAUSE.

DOCTORS AND DIAGNOSIS

Medicine and Sexual Abuse

One of the tragedies of the Cleveland case was that a great debate consumed a community that was neither consulted nor enlightened about the technical terminology. A kind of *fatwa* silenced the professionals. But in the autumn of 1987, when Elizabeth Butler-Sloss was beginning her judicial inquiry, child protection managers in Nottinghamshire tried to democratise the debate. They organised a special Parliamentary briefing and presented a panel of doctors, police, social workers and academics, introduced by Professor Olive Stevenson, to explain to an audience of MPs the new knowledge about abuse. Along one side sat Middlesbrough's Labour MP, Stuart Bell, flanked by a team of Tories. That alliance was to define the colour of the crusade.

The Nottinghamshire child protection team had called the meeting to say: look at our figures; we have correlated cases which combined forensic evidence with similar signs, supported by young children's stories about abuse by their fathers or father-figures. A paediatrician from Leeds, Dr Jane Wynne, showed slides of the raw and palpably painful bottoms and genitals of some of their patients. Bell and his crusaders shuffled papers, whispered to each other and fidgeted like bad lads at the back of the class. The rest looked and listened in stillness. After they'd finished the Tory MP Richard Holt asked how he could understand the anal dilatation sign – colloquially, a gaping anus – at the heart of the Cleveland controversy. Anal dilatation had somehow acquired the status of magic; it had entered popular discourse and yet few understood what it was.

'Do I have to be a doctor to understand the validity?' he asked. 'Could you tell me how to do it . . .?'

'I wouldn't,' replied Dr Wynne.

The Honourable Gentleman's dyspepsia was manifest. 'Why not? Can you teach me to do it?'

'Well, of course, you can transfer skills . . .' ventured Dr Wynne hesitantly.

'I'm sure she could teach you to recognise enlarged tonsils,' someone else suggested.

Poor Mr Holt's temper was understandable. Like the rest of us, he wanted to know exactly what the magic sign meant. He appeared to want the culture of common sense to understand the so-called 'test' which had been flashed in front of our eyes, only to be spirited away again in the hieroglyphics which the experts alone could decipher. Holt's demand at least articulated a populist revolt against what were represented as evangelising experts who kept their signs a secret. But was it the experts who kept *sexual abuse* a secret? Or was it the system of sexual politics sustained by Holt et al.?

But that was exactly Dr Wynne's point. This wasn't a magic test; it was only a simple sign. Perhaps the problem was what the sign signified – something *in* society rather than *outside* it, something we could, but would not, see. Anal dilatation, moreover, was not a test: it wasn't something doctors did to children. It was a sign, the activity of

16

an anus. By gaping open, it signalled that it might have been penetrated.

Sexual abuse of women and children had been brought to the political agenda in the 1970s and 1980s by the modern women's movement. However, in 1987 sexual abuse became associated not with a movement but with 'experts', paediatricians who had expanded their concern with non-accidental injury to the sexual abuse of children. Political movements and experts are, of course, pariahs in the ideology of Thatcherism, but where the former derive from popular feelings and objectives, the latter are vulnerable in their social isolation from the 'base, common and popular'. Their professional discourses have contained them within professional networks rather than social alliances. Long before the Cleveland volcano erupted, social workers and doctors (along with teachers, polytechnic lecturers and sociologists) had been specifically maligned by Thatcherism. Not only were they naughty experts but, like the women's movement, they committed the social crime of trespassing across the hallowed threshold of the family.

The Leeds discovery

Dr Wynne and her colleague Dr Christopher Hobbs didn't invent sexual abuse or anal dilatation. Their innovation was that they reached a diagnosis that was well known in another branch of medicine – forensic pathology – to paediatrics. For the first time the science of sexual crime was applied to the world of children. The result was dramatic. 'Baby battering' had become a child health issue in the 1960s and '70s. In the 1980s their detection of one kind of abuse – violence – led them to another – sex, and within a couple of years they were having more children referred to them for suspected sexual abuse than for other forms of ill-treatment. Like battering, sexual abuse was becoming a public health issue, a matter of prevention rather than punishment. In 1985–86, police and social services referred 1,368 children suspected of being abused or neglected; of these, 608 were thought to have been sexually abused.

Leeds consultant paediatrician Dr Michael Buchanan is an iconoclast whose slightly bawdy talk disguises a fastidious commitment to children and to scholarship. 'I'm not very shockable but I am shocked by pictures of abused children. For anyone there in the front line it builds up and up until you need to have a good scream.'

Dr Buchanan had long worked on non-accidental injuries with his two younger consultants, Drs Wynne and Hobbs, and they were alerted in the 1980s to American research on sexual abuse by Jill McMurray, who held the city's 'children at risk' register.

'These Americans began writing on this years ago, and we said to ourselves, "It's not like that in Leeds, there's a bit of incest here and there, but that's normal." You know what happens: disbelief and denial. But emissaries began to arrive here and I sent one of our people to America – around 1982 we were seeing between two and five cases of sexual abuse a year. But as each year went by our figures seemed to double. We had a sexual explosion. In medicine, when your eyes are open there's a great risk that you begin to *see*. It's ever so easy. The thing was, we weren't looking up the anal canal – we'd only given it a passing glance.

'But you'd begin to get clues. You'd have an alerted eye. You'd start to look at the vulva and anus in the same way as you'd look at ears and throats. At one time if a child said, "My dad put his hand in my knickers," people would say, "Filthy little liar." We've got countless files of children who *tried* to tell. Modesty applies – among the children and the doctors. There was disinterest: why should you look? What would you see? When I say we didn't look, I mean we only gave it a passing glance, but never did we remember seeing gaping anuses. You get clues, and now and again you'd see something odd like a discharge, soreness, a bruise in a funny place, on the vulva itself perhaps, or on the penis, and the anus, of course – there's a whole lot of signs, but one of them is that *it's gaping at you, because something big has been in it.*

'Disbelief began to evaporate. We read articles, went to meetings, and then after the second or fourth case it began to make sense. And then things would happen like someone writing about, say, five boys among 100 girls, and you think, "Oh, boys!" We're expecting the number of boys and girls to equalise.

'A child's vagina is not made for abuse, it doesn't dilate. So for abusers who want orifices the anus is the place. They've been at it for years. Abusers will abuse anything holes in the floor, their own children, anybody else's, anyone or anything.'

In the 1970s Buchanan's consciousness had also been raised by reading feminist texts like Shere Hitc's studies of adult sexual relationships. 'I wasn't personally aware of the pressure women felt and all those for whom there was no pleasure in sex at all. It was shattering. Sex was designed for chaps. Male attitudes play a major part in abuse: pressure, coercion and threats.'

The sexual abuse work was galvanised by Jane Wynne and Chris Hobbs, both of them experienced and senior paediatricians, who appeared to navigate the etiquette of the medical Establishment while making paediatric – and political – waves. They put themselves into a rare process for consultants, raising consciousness with other professionals who would be regarded as subordinate in the medical hierarchy. In a working group they encouraged a collegial culture among professionals to contemplate physical signs and they explored the implications of anal abuse, both professionally and personally.

Dr Wynne recalled being urged by her hospital's forensic scientist Michael Green to look at bottoms on the grounds that at least 10 per cent of heterosexual adults practised anal intercourse. 'So we looked. The thing was that at the start we saw a lot of very young children being referred to us by nursery nurses etc., and they'd been anally abused. Or we saw a girl with vaginal discharge and then we'd notice other signs as well, examine the other children in the family and find that they'd been abused too. So, we accepted that it happened, and that it happened to boys and girls. And you couldn't necessarily rely on the retrospective information from adults. Women telling us about abuse in their own childhood don't usually talk about oral or anal sex. Part of the problem with anal abuse is that maybe it happened under five years of age, and then it changed to the vagina. The other important distinction between adults and children is that the forensic work is really only important for acute sexual assault – rape. But child abuse is chronic, it's different. So really we were all on the wrong tack.

'Chris Hobbs and I were relatively senior, so we'd seen a lot of children and we'd good knowledge of what "normal" is, so we were in a good position to recognise that what we were seeing wasn't normal. We set up a working party which met monthly or weekly on sexual abuse, so we got used to talking about sex and children in a very relaxed way. We were slow to start with. We knew that out there, there were all these children who we weren't seeing and we were worried about it because we didn't know if we would recognise it or be able to handle it.'

They first familiarised themselves with the literature and with the forensic skills, like taking swabs for evidence – what Dr Wynne calls 'bot swabs etc.'. They worked closely with the police and the courts. And the working group shared their experience in seminars with others working with children, ranging from social workers to nursery nurses. They were open to anyone with a worry. That genesis made Leeds among the most abuse-conscious cities in Britain, a consciousness that was regularly affirmed by social services chairman Councillor Bernard Atha, and the city council.

However, the discovery for which they became famous – their detection of anal dilatation as a common sign of buggery – wasn't new. 'Our claim to fame was just that we were looking at *children's* bots. Bingo, we saw a variety of different signs. We knew about normal bottoms, we knew about laxity, we knew about fissures and anal dilatation. And the children were telling us at the same time that they'd been hurt in their bottoms. We worked with the sexually explicit dollies and were getting a lot of feedback from the children, and actually we had quite a few perpetrators telling us as well,' said Dr Wynne.

Although forensic pathologists and police surgeons had written about anal dilatation for many years, Drs Wynne and Hobbs were the first to identify and then measure its appearance in children, and then to infer that buggery was a *significant* feature of child sex abuse.

According to Jill McMurray, the sharing of knowledge encouraged referrals by carers of young children, including, significantly, nursery staff, and by mothers. Their vigilance changed both the age and gender profile of victims: as the average age dropped to seven-and-a-half years by 1987, so the balance of the genders began to even up to around one boy for every two girls. This contradicted the very low proportion of boys revealed in surveys based on adults' retrospective disclosures. What the team also uncovered were entirely unexpected signs of penetration among primary school children, toddlers and even babies of both sexes.

Dr Wynne and Dr Hobbs published a pioneering paper, 'Buggery in Childhood – A Common Syndrome of Child Abuse', in the prestigious medical journal, the *Lancet*, on 4 October 1986, reporting that not only had the number of sexually abused children coming to their attention surpassed battered children, but 'anorectal abuse of young children is more common than the battered-child syndrome in this age group . . . we have become aware of more cases of anal abuse than of any other forms of sexual abuse in very young children of both sexes.'

This was shocking. More children were being buggered than battered.

In only half a year they reported seeing 35 cases of buggery among 17 boys and 18 girls under 14 years. Importantly, over two-thirds of these were under-fives. It was devastating data. If it was true, it detonated the popular myth of the Lolitas whose budding bodies incited helpless stepfathers.

All the children in their study displayed abnormalities of the anus, half of them reported interference with their bottoms by adults, and in a handful of other cases brothers or sisters provided the history. All the cases carried corroboration of the diagnosis by disclosures, admissions by perpetrators, reports from nurseries, police, foster parents, schools or social workers. A third of the perpetrators were the biological fathers. Most of the rest were stepfathers or trusted men in the children's world.

Dr Wynne recalled that it was the testimonies of the children themselves which urged them to look at the anus.

'A 12-year-old girl suddenly began wetting and was a bit sad. The school nurse organised a medical and she was taken to social services and then we saw her. She was very red at the front. I said, "I'm sorry, you'd better tell me about it." Her dad had been buggering her three times a week for six years.' The evidence? When the child relaxed, a gaping anus.

'Having recognised the physical indications of such abuse and related them to statements by the children or siblings, we are in no doubt that it is a common form of abuse which so far seems to have escaped detection – largely because of doctors' lack of awareness and failure to examine the anus,' said the *Lancet* article. There was no magic test which conjured sights hitherto unseen. Wynne and Hobbs simply said: listen to the child, and when they say something's been in their bum they mean their bum, not somewhere else!

'As vaginal intercourse is uncommon in girls under five,' they wrote, 'we must conclude that anal intercourse is the usual form of peri-anal intercourse in both sexes. Our experience is that boys and girls seem to be at similar risk of this type of abuse.'

The younger the child, it seems, the more the gender of the victim is a matter of indifference to the abuser.

Paediatricians began to speculate in public on the dynamics of a bit of the body hitherto confined to lavatorial kiddie-talk, dirty-talk and technical-talk of specialists. What were the dynamics of the anus, they asked each other? What was the precise mechanism that caused dilatation? Was it the body's response to penetration? Did it allow the anus to *receive* something coming up rather than down, in rather than out, repeatedly, without rendering it incontinent. And why the anus? Because the vagina, the supposedly natural home of the penis, was simply too small. 'If you tried to penetrate a little girl's vagina with an adult penis, you'd rip the child from stem to stern,' explained Dr Wynne. The anus was infinitely more accommodating.

The paper provoked a swift rebuke from Manchester police surgeon Dr Raine Roberts, who insisted that bum didn't necessarily mean bum. 'Many of the histories given are very vague. Children of all ages may refer to their "bottom" or "bum" when they mean any part of their genitalia, and even older children's knowledge of their anatomy may be inadequate,' she replied in the *Lancet* on 8 November 1986. 'It is very easy to pull on the buttocks and produce photographs which show apparent fissures and slackness of the sphincter,' she added. This was an argument that was later repudiated at the Cleveland inquiry by her Manchester colleague, Dr Frank Bamford, a Reader in Paediatrics.

In the same issue, in which Drs Wynne and Hobbs were invited to reply to Dr Roberts, they wondered what happened to the 21 children referred to her in 1986 with a history of anal interference, when she found evidence only among six. 'We are concerned about the 21 children who have a history of anal abuse in Roberts' series; were they believed? Research shows that children rarely lie about sexual abuse.'

Wynne and Hobbs published a second paper in the *Lancet* on 10 October 1987 which revealed signs of anal penetration among around half of 337 cases of sexual abuse confirmed in 1985–86.

Tyneside: a new consciousness

While the Leeds consultants were trawling their data in the early 1980s and finding new evidence of buggery among children, doctors in other cities working with adult rape survivors found themselves with a totally unexpected category of clients – children. Although they were apparently on different trajectories, all these doctors were moving towards similar discoveries. And all of them were travelling the rough road that led to Cleveland.

After the showing in 1983 of the television documentary by Roger Graef, which exposed harassment of a rape survivor by Thames Valley detectives, the Home Office circularised all police forces to encourage them to make women officers available to deal with sexual offences. Northumbria police force, for example, together with Tyneside's Rape Crisis Centre, that year conceived the idea of recruiting a group of women doctors to examine the victims of sexual crimes. Some of them were trained by Newcastle's redoubtable paediatric consultant, the late Christine Cooper, who had already built up an international reputation with her work on all forms of child abuse. She alerted her colleagues to sexual abuse including buggery.

One of the doctors she helped to train was Dr Ellis Fraser, a retired family planning doctor, who joined the Tyneside Women Police Doctors Group after she had seen the programme on the Thames Valley police. She was to become in her late sixties a specialist in sexual abuse.

'I'd retired a little earlier, and I thought this was something I could and should do, because I felt it would be easier for a woman to be examined by a woman. Two or three a year we'd see, that's what the police surgeons said to us. Within weeks we were being asked to see children. Examining a rape victim was well within the scope of any woman who'd been in general practice or family planning, but children was a very different thing. We were highly alarmed. Even the paediatricians amongst us weren't sure what the genitalia of little girls looked like. Only seven or eight of us were prepared to do it. We got Christine Cooper to come and help and every time we saw a child we met together, but we found it very difficult to get information.'

Usually, said Dr Fraser, a doctor could resort to a textbook, but they didn't help. 'This was a mystery. We learned an awful lot from each other and from the police sergeant and the young policewomen in their child protection units. The police gave us great encouragement.'

In the first year she saw eight children. Within three years she alone was seeing over 100 a year – a total of nearly 400 by the end of 1987, including nearly 40 cases of suspected buggery.

One of her young colleagues in Newcastle, Dr Lesley Duke, reckoned that, 'Because of the police work we're getting skills we didn't have before, we're becoming specialists. We were shocked and appalled at first, because we all had a stereotype of an incest survivor as a 14- or 15-year-old runaway. Abused children are very protective of adults, they're responsible for the whole family. I'm sure buggery is much more common than we think. Children can't talk about "it" so they disclose less. It's been concealed, and we've been hoodwinked by the kids. Unless you talk to other people, you get on the wrong track. It's been so much a question of *looking*. Bottoms haven't been looked at because it's too awful to contemplate.'

But looked at for what? Another member of Tyneside Women Police Doctors Group, Dr Charlotte Wright, recalled that, 'There's a truism in all the books, that penetrative intercourse is very rare in children under six or seven. But that's because they weren't looking, or they were just looking in the wrong orifice. Buggery is the hardest thing to contemplate because it is the ultimately impossible act. I recall seeing one little girl, she said, "It hurts in my bottom." The doctor said it was her vagina. But it wasn't, it was her bottom. The trouble was, we had extrapolated downwards – sex doesn't go on in bottoms. But once you do see it, it hits you in the eye. When the Tyneside Women Police Doctors Group went for training we were told we'd not see much anal dilatation. And we were not trained to *look* at genitalia. We were taught to feel, put our fingers in. But nobody ever said, this is a clitoris, etc., because there's a feeling that it's rude, and that there's no need to examine genitalia until people are sexually active. So none of us had seen children's hymens before.'

Within a couple of years, though, Dr Fraser became an expert on the shape and size of girls' hymens, which gave her a considerable reputation for rigour and vigilance. But nothing had prepared the group culturally, medically or psychologically for the swathe of children the Tyneside police were presenting to them. Only the consciousness-raising mode of their small group sustained some trust in their own perceptions, especially after the impact of Cleveland began to terrify their colleagues and the courts elsewhere. At least the detection of sexual abuse on Tyneside had an extraordinary alliance wrapped around it: the women doctors, the police, and Tyneside Rape Crisis Centre (TRCC), whose profile of clients during the 1980s had changed significantly: 60 per cent of clients come to disclose abuse in their own childhood. 'The women doctors' scheme developed magnificently,' said the TRCC, 'we certainly know the difference between before and after.'

The alliance organised their own re-education. The doctors called a conference in 1983 and invited Manchester's Dr Raine Roberts, who had travelled similar tracks by challenging the police on their treatment of rape victims in the mid-1970s and becoming the city's premier police surgeon handling the victims of sexual offences.

Initially more than 30 doctors were involved and there was a worry that they would not gain enough experience. The work has subsequently devolved to around seven or eight who now have considerable expertise.

Most of the Tynesiders' cases were referred by the police, and they learned to look for buggery from Christine Cooper. 'Buggery does produce that sign. We always said somebody might find other reasons, but we do know that buggery is one reason. It became obvious that it was the commonest reason,' said Dr Fraser. 'If you keep a child in hospital you can eliminate other neurological features known to paediatricians. Nurses know to watch if a child is constipated, because minor degrees of dilatation can be caused by chronic constipation. But you can feel a loaded colon, so nurses know what to watch for.'

The Tynesiders' first source of academic support came with the publication of Jane Wynne and Christopher Hobbs' pioneering paper. 'When we first read it we thought they must have funny kids in Leeds,' said Dr Wright, but nevertheless the consultant paediatricians were reporting on *young* children and this provided the first scholarly vindication of the Tynesiders' own experience.

Over the sea to Ireland

It was the great debate exploding around the treatment of rape victims which brought the police and women doctors in the Republic of Ireland together to form a special Sexual Assault Treatment Unit in Dublin, initiated by another family planning specialist, Dr Moira Woods. For some time she had been sent victims of sexual offences by the Rape Crisis Centre and the police, since there is no equivalent in the Republic of Ireland of Britain's police surgeons. By 1984 Dr Woods was also being sent children: other doctors, apparently, didn't want the hassle of making difficult pronouncements and defending them in court.

That year the Minister of Health appointed a working party on rape, and after a year agreed to set up a national specialist unit attached to the Rotunda maternity hospital. The unit opened in 1985. Before the year was out it was receiving more children than adults – 50 new cases of child sexual abuse every month, a total of 1,500 in two years.

'We're open to anyone 24 hours a day on a rota system. Every time there's a television programme on child abuse we get more mothers ringing up, whereas before they had no method of getting to us without being screened by others, which meant the poor child had to keep telling its story over and over,' said Dr Woods.

And the unit saw anal abuse immediately. 'We *looked* in every child. We had to because some children would tell you that he stuck something in their bum. But a lot of them, the very frightened ones, won't tell you anything. We looked because we were not going to miss *anything*. And children aren't going to tell you, a total stranger, everything on the first interview. Of course they're not: why should they?

'I knew from seeing an enormous number of adults over ten years that in this country the number of women subjected to rectal abuse is incredible. I had one incest case who'd had two children by her father. She came for a cervical smear. We talked a lot and to my amazement she knew nothing, no memory of the births, and only when I showed her drawings of different parts of the body did she say she now realised that "that's where he put it" and it was her bum. A little girl was four days in hospital with vaginal bleeding, looked at by four doctors. I asked her, "What are

you in hospital for?" and she said, "My bum is bleeding."
I asked, "What made your bum bleed?", and she said,
"He stuck his willy in my bum." Nobody had asked her.'

Dr Woods remembered another little girl who 'bounced
in and said, "My dad hurt my bummy and made it bleed."
Straight out. Her eight-year-old sister just sat; no, she said,
"Everything at home is lovely, Mummy is lovely, Daddy is
lovely." I examined her – I could put two fingers in her
vagina and her rectum dilated up to an inch. I said maybe
there was something she forgot to tell me. She said, "Yep".
It took me 18 months to find out what that something
was. She cried and cried. She only agreed to say who'd
hurt her if she wrote it on a piece of paper and if I
promised to tear it up. It said "Daddy". I tore it up. She
had her head on my lap, and cried and cried. Don't
assume for one minute that the children have told you
everything. They always keep back the worst things.'

Meanwhile in Manchester

The Tyneside, Dublin and Leeds doctors developed their
work independently, at least initially, but came up with
similar results. Manchester police set up a Sexual Assault
Treatment Unit, run by Dr Raine Roberts, who was to
become the most vocal opponent of the anal dilatation
thesis in Cleveland and in courts up and down the country
in 1987. This unit, too, saw large numbers of children.
These centres were seeing *more* children than anywhere
else and their data must, therefore, be taken as deriving
from best current practice.

Two features stand out from the data gathered in Leeds,
Tyneside and Dublin. Leeds, the pioneers in diagnosing
anal abuse, continued to discover much higher levels of
buggery than anywhere else – an expression of detection
rather than incidence. Manchester diagnosed much lower

levels of anal abuse than Leeds, Tyneside and Dublin. Of 608 referrals confirmed in Leeds, 337 showed anal signs. Among boys this represented 83 per cent; among girls 25 per cent.

The Leeds children showed significant age and gender variations in the prevalence of anal abuse. Anal penetration was more common than vaginal penetration among the youngest girls, but this ratio reversed by puberty. There are no comparable figures elsewhere in Britain, but data from Tyneside, Dr Fraser and Dublin show anal signs in more than 8 per cent of confirmed cases. Only Dr Roberts and Manchester's unit were diagnosing much lower rates of anal abuse.

	Cases confirmed	*Anal signs*
Dublin Rotunda	530	8%
Tyneside	224	8%
Ellis Fraser	317	9.4%
Raine Roberts	103	3.8%
Greater Manchester Sexual Assault Unit	879	3%

Drs Wynne and Hobbs' request for more data from Dr Roberts after her combative letter to the *Lancet* was never followed up. The judicial inquiry into the Cleveland crisis likewise made repeated requests to Dr Roberts to provide data, to enable comparison with the other expert evidence offered from Tyneside and Yorkshire. This was important – Dr Roberts had launched a crusade against them, after all. She never delivered the data.

Raine Roberts was a general practitioner who also got into child sexual abuse through her work on rape. In the 1970s she had skirmished with Manchester police and the

Police Surgeons Association over their treatment of raped women. She had written on rape for the *Police Surgeons Manual*, and by the 1980s was Manchester's primary police surgeon dealing with sexual offences. That was what brought her to the attention of the Tyneside Women Police Doctors Group, who invited her to address their 1983 conference. 'We asked her to come because we'd read her chapter in the *Police Surgeons Manual*,' said Dr Fraser, 'but she wasn't very helpful, she was very aggressive in the way she spoke, not in any way encouraging. She didn't want to come or to encourage us. I don't know why she was so very hostile to anybody else trying to do this work.'

This was confirmed by retired Northumbria Superintendent, Rhona Cross. 'Her contribution was destructive and not always accurate. I bear that in mind now, because perhaps she didn't have the expertise of Dr Wynne in Leeds. She wasn't helpful, so we were a bit unhappy. She was rather contemptuous of the Women Police Doctors Group.'

In her own city, Dr Roberts seemed to work well with the police but had little or no connection with the women's organisations emerging among the survivors of sex crime in the city. Manchester set up the country's first Sexual Assault Referral Centre at St Mary's Hospital in 1986. It was run by Dr Roberts. The working group which planned the centre included representatives from the police, police surgeons and the health authority, but there was no one from the women's organisations in the voluntary sector which were actually working with abused women – Manchester Rape Crisis Centre, the Saheli Asian Women's Refuge, and Taboo, the incest survivors' group. They all had a critique of the location and priorities of the centre once it was opened.

Dr Roberts was among the police surgeons called in by

Cleveland lawyers representing fathers during the 1987 crisis and after. She came to be seen as an itinerant vigilante ready to appear as an expert witness in courts all over the country to challenge the evidence of anal signs. By the end of the year she appeared to have lined herself up with the disbelievers in contrast to her challenge to the police establishment in the 1970s.

The Cleveland saga

The arrival of Dr Marietta Higgs at Middlesbrough General Hospital in January 1987 did not inaugurate Cleveland's concern with child sexual abuse. The saga really started some years earlier, with efforts by health visitors Marjorie Dunn and Freda Roach to prepare the county, morally and materially. They were to find an important source of support in Sue Richardson, who was appointed child abuse consultant in 1986 – but strangely enough, not in Dr Higgs or her colleague Dr Geoffrey Wyatt, an energetic young consultant at Middlesbrough General.

It began for Marjorie Dunn, a softly spoken Scotswoman who was an experienced health visitor, in 1983, when she and Freda Roach were appointed nursing officers with designated responsibility for child sexual abuse. Apart from attending to the usual, and growing, pressure of individual cases and case conferences, the two women were promoting education on sexual abuse among schools, nurses, mothers – and doctors. Marjorie Dunn's story was never really told to the Cleveland inquiry. Hers was an independent voice, and it was as if all the corporate interests represented there conspired to silence it.

The year 1983 was for her, like many others, a turning point. She had attended a Teesside Polytechnic seminar on sexual abuse and heard the challenging, not to say provocative, testimonies of women from Cleveland Rape Crisis Centre.

'I remember one policeman was there saying it made him think of all the runaway kids the police picked up every weekend. It was a watershed for me because I added to it what I already knew about adults. I came away feeling ashamed that I'd been health visiting for eight years and never came across it in a single family. I'd talked to adults about it and yet never made the connection that any of my nice families were doing this sort of thing.

'Because awareness was growing, by 1985 we were having to make it a special category in our abuse records. That's why it was so annoying to hear it said that it all started on 1 May 1987. Actually, that seemed like an interruption to our work, it blotted out everything we had done.'

Marjorie Dunn had thought doctors should look at children's bottoms *before* she read the Wynne and Hobbs paper in the *Lancet*, and before she came across the anal dilatation diagnosis, because she was drawing on her knowledge of the need to look for signs on battered children. 'After 1983 the more we thought about it the more we made the links. I wasn't thinking about anal dilatation, I'd never heard of it. But because of my experience as a health visitor with child abuse I thought there should be some signs apparent to the eye, and I was thinking there might just be signs around the anus – bruises, that kind of thing. And if you've got the privilege of looking at the whole child in medical examinations then you should see it as a whole entity. Bottoms are part of the child, so I suggested they look at the anus and the genitals for some signs.

'This is what I suggested to doctors and the paediatricians in our informal conversations about cases. We never really managed to get them to meetings because they were so busy, and it was difficult for them to see that it would be useful. But we'd mention it at times when we were discussing co-ordination and co-operation on individual cases. But there wasn't a lot of interest, they were fairly patronising. You see, there's a lack of respect for our knowledge. Things never really worked very well between us and paediatricians, because it's about the difference between consultants and nurses, who aren't seen to be important. We were told, "Look, dear" (they always say "dear"), "we're so busy, child abuse is the whole of your job, but it is a tiny part of my job and I can't get involved, I've got so many sick children to look after." That was fair comment, to say they couldn't start worrying about bums when they were looking after children who were dying. But the more I work with it, the more I see it being linked with child health in its fullness. I find that attitude quite insulting, because it devalues children. Paediatricians are in the right position to deal with the whole child – that's what we pay them for.'

The health visitors organised meetings and training sessions and a couple of paediatricians from Middlesbrough General turned up, Dr Isobel Grant and Dr Peter Morrell – but not Dr Geoffrey Wyatt.

Dr Wyatt may not have been interested in the health visitors' expertise on child abuse, but he did have grand plans of his own which gained little support in the area, though they provided a clue to his bravura. He wanted children out of hospital and nursing provided for them at home, and he appeared to think that health visitors might have an important place in this project. The health visitors were quick to explain that it was their job not to *cure* illness but to try to *prevent* it. He pressed the point that they could be part of his team. But they already had their own team, they said, and furthermore they were already working well with mothers. They could do the same work for him, he suggested. But they wanted to do it for the area not for him, they said. 'It's back to us women. We are supposed to be the malleable followers of the leaders,' said one of them.

Dr Wyatt's community plan also irritated the South Tees Community Health Council, which was later to throw itself behind the parents' rebellion against the Middlesbrough paediatricians in 1987. Dr Wyatt was universally acknowledged to be a good, caring doctor. He was well known for working late into the night and some feared that his infinite energy and curiosity might sooner or later become burnt out. But he seemed to become a marked man after a revolt against cuts imposed by hospital management.

Middlesbrough General Hospital is situated in one of the poorest communities in England. Professor Peter Townsend's 1986 report, *Inequalities in Health in the Northern Region*, also found it to be one of the sickest even within this ailing region. This report not only measured ill-health by death rates, but factored children into the equation by adding low birth weights. Middlesbrough, together with a couple of other Cleveland areas, ranked among those with the highest proportion of children with low birth weight. According to one of the Middlesbrough Hospital doctors, there was already bad blood between the General's management and paediatrics. At the beginning of the 1980s the hospital had 150 paediatric beds; by 1987 it had only 52. In the winter before the child abuse crisis, the children's wards were already overflowing: a bronchitis epidemic packed in *more* children than the sexual abuse diagnosis.

Nursing staff were already exhausted when child abuse admissions rocketed in May.

The nursing officer for Ward 9, Iris Chambers, told the Cleveland inquiry that in February she had already been so worried about the pressure on nurses that she wrote to the Director of Nursing Services to complain about nurses having to do extra duties. Dr Wyatt was a vocal protagonist in the continuing protests against cuts. 'We reckon we need 80 beds on this site,' said one of Dr Wyatt's colleagues. 'We've been campaigning fairly hard to improve things – so there's a history of aggro. Dr Wyatt was a thorn in the management's side because he never stopped campaigning to increase the services for children. Dr Higgs was the same. So we've always been at the administrators' throats to improve services.'

Dr Higgs arrived with none of that history, although she quickly became associated with 'troublemakers', defending standards and services and, more than that, adding child abuse to the hospital's agenda. Marjorie Dunn recalled Dr Higgs' arrival and how 'we spent time with her, because we'd grab anyone who showed an interest. She was much more aware of the possibility of looking at the whole child, and of looking at bums. She shared our viewpoint.'

Dr Higgs is an Australian who has spent most of her working life in British hospitals, moving with her family between the south and the north as her career progressed – 'It is quite a nomadic business being a junior doctor in this country,' she said. She normally worked until after 8 p.m., and well into the wee small hours when on call. In the early 1980s she had worked with Christine Cooper, a formative influence on services for abused children, and shared her commitment to keeping families together wherever possible. In 1982 she went to neighbouring Gateshead where her work expanded to include more child abuse training and therapeutic work with children. During that stint she met a child who left a lasting mark on her mind.

The nine-year-old girl had been abused by her step-father and teenage brother. Dr Higgs and the child met fortnightly for a year, with the child sitting on a rafter over a window in the Victorian clinic. 'I do not think I ever, even in that length of time, managed to begin to form a relationship with this child,' Dr Higgs told the inquiry. The nearest she felt she got to showing the child that people could care was a conversation in which the child spent 'the entire session asking who would care, what would happen if she threw herself from the window, what would I do, would I care, what would the secretaries downstairs do. And that was after a year . . . It was a very sobering experience for me to have met that child.'

While at Tyneside she also learned to take forensic swabs, in the event of cases being prosecuted by the police, and worked with specialist police units who would come to hospitals and take statements from doctors. That would have helped in Cleveland, she told the inquiry.

Her first case of sexual abuse was in February, when a police surgeon, Dr Joyce Longwill, contacted Sue Richardson to share her worries about a child she had seen in a school clinic. When Sue Richardson proposed calling in a police surgeon – a doctor who also does an extra police rota – Dr Longwill explained that she was one her-self, and so she suggested Dr Higgs instead. Senior Police Surgeon Alastair Irvine joined them to supervise the exam-ination and appeared to agree that there were suspicious signs of sexual abuse, although he was later to refuse offi-cially to endorse their findings.

Only a handful of sexual abuse cases joined Dr Higgs' workload before May. The majority of the 78 cases she diagnosed, and which came under the inquiry's scrutiny, emerged between May and June. The explosion was partly explained, she suggested, by the large networks of siblings or close relatives involved with the 44 children originally diagnosed. Only eight of her diagnoses rested on anal dilatation alone. The volume was also partly explained by the number of undiagnosed cases which had appeared in outpatients' clinics for some time. It seemed to be a combination of her own vigilance, large families and children's networks, and a backlog which had accumulated in outpatients.

Dr Higgs was accused by parents and by counsel during the inquiry of examining children's bottoms when she gave children routine general examinations. What her interrogators revealed, by implication, was that children's bottoms had *not* normally been examined. Which is worse? To see, or not to look?

And why had she been looking at bottoms? In some cases, nurses had drawn her attention to abnormal signs. In others, Dr Higgs included bottoms as part of her routine examination of children with conditions increasingly associated with sexual abuse. During the controversy, much was made of children going in with asthma and being kept in for sexual abuse. Actually, there was only one child with asthma, who had been referred to the paediatrician after a hospital registrar noticed anal abnormalities in any case. Why was any of this unusual?

Marjorie Dunn thought it shouldn't be unusual, but revealed the barrage of resistance. 'I am still amazed at the criticism we get from our own colleagues. They say it's *rude*, they say you shouldn't do it without parental permission. But why shouldn't it be the same as the routine examination of ears or tonsils? It's not that I have no thought to modesty, but the question is, how do children and adults perceive them? Children feel they're just another bit of their bodies. It's adults who have the modesty, who think that bottoms, and sex, are rude.'

Controversial practices

Dr Wyatt explained in his evidence to the judicial inquiry that not only had he not seen signs but that he had misread the signs in patients who had returned to his care many, many times. Working with Dr Higgs encouraged him to recognise that, 'I had been consistently missing obvious signs of sexual abuse, and hence that I had not been offering the children the care they deserve.' This produced not a 'crude determination to avoid missing sexual abuse at all costs, but a determination to consider sexual abuse as a possible diagnosis'. He came to feel that his previous failure was nothing less than 'a questionable and controversial practice'. When he became aware of Dr Irvine's implacable hostility to the anal dilatation thesis, he concluded that the contentious issue was not 'the interpretation of these signs but whether or not these signs were being recognised and acted upon'.

Dr Wyatt came across his first case of abuse almost immediately after his appointment at Middlesbrough in 1983, when he noticed a vulval tear in a six-month-old girl. He interpreted this as non-accidental injury, although a man was later jailed after admitting to the police that he had sexually abused this baby girl. Dr Wyatt later believed that this typified the response to sexual abuse – it was non-accidental injury with an occasional sexual dimension.

Dr Wyatt made his first diagnosis of suspected sexual abuse in April, a case in which a child disclosed that it had been abused. In May he began to re-think his earlier assumptions about children who were making one of their many return visits to his clinics – now he saw signs which he interpreted as consistent with sexual abuse. Some sub-sequently confirmed his findings with disclosures that they had been abused.

When tackled about the perception that he was thrilled with his new discoveries, he explained in his evidence to the inquiry that he was 'bound to feel professional satis-faction when I found evidence which helps to explain the cause of a child's condition'.

By May the paediatricians were admitting many more children to the ward, not least to protect children while their cases were investigated. The pressure forced staff to move some children to adult wards – though not for the first time. Children had been shifted to other wards during the bronchiolitis epidemic earlier that year. But when camp beds were hauled into Ward 9 and some children were billeted among adults elsewhere, Nursing Officer Iris Chambers complained to Dr Higgs about their numbers. Nurses felt both exhausted and excluded; they felt nobody was consulting them properly about what was going on. During the weekend of 13–14 June, Iris Chambers tackled Dr Higgs again, saying that the ward was full. By 20 June, the paediatricians had been asked to reduce the rate of admissions, and after they said they could not, they met with hospital and social services managers who again urged them to slow down: if not, then at least they should be mindful that dissent was rumbling around the district health authority. After the paediatricians were later accused of empire-building, Dr Wyatt replied that, 'A great need has existed in this very deprived part of the country for a long time'. He would not compromise a child's health and welfare 'by turning a blind eye to that child's problems simply to save resources'.

Nevertheless, there was already a crisis of resources, which had been exposed during the winter epidemic. And

Iris Chambers was not alone in feeling that the ward was not an appropriate place for sexually abused children. She told the inquiry that when she tackled Dr Higgs again about the overcrowding and complained that the nurses could not cope, 'She said, "I agree with you. You must get more nurses."'

Tension between nurses and Dr Higgs came to be symbolised in their different uses of a small room which housed emergency equipment. It also had a bed and a desk, and increasingly Dr Higgs moved the bed away from the door to provide privacy for any child being examined. But nurses found themselves rushing in with a child urgently needing to be attached to a drip, only to find that the drip and the bed were now at opposite ends of the room. According to one nurse, who did not give evidence at the inquiry, 'the hierarchy was a lot less on Ward 9 than elsewhere, but when people complained she [Dr Higgs] seemed to ignore it. She regarded what she was doing as a higher priority. She had to make long telephone calls to social workers, but she didn't have her own office at the General, so that caused hassle. People were resentful that she'd started something and now we were *all* in this terrible mess. I remember the May Bank Holiday. None of these children were ill and they treated the ward like a playgroup, going out on bikes, playing with their parents – and we had to amuse them for 18 hours a day. They'd play with the traction or play, literally, under the bed of a very sick child. It was like the Bash Street kids.'

Nurses also had to cope with distressed children in the wake of disclosures they wanted to retract. 'We didn't know what to do. Children liked her [Dr Higgs]; they weren't afraid of going to see her and I found that she always explained to them what she was going to do. She was much more approachable among children, they could see her any time, she'd not snap or ignore them, like doctors who might be politely rejecting or just a bit curt.

'But we found it hard to get information from her on how long the children would be staying or what to do with them. They needed supervision. It was a nightmare. You had a lot of "free" children, and if you didn't look after them they ran riot. She had taken over the bricks and mortar of the ward, but we needed the ward for physically and mentally ill children. I think she shouldn't have started something until she had the resources and support. I believe what she is doing is right, but she didn't prepare any ground. None of us nurses would disagree that sexual abuse happens, but we needed information on how to talk to children, we wanted practical guidelines.'

And in this respect Dr Higgs' behaviour seemed to reveal more about her profession than her personality. She seems to have behaved no differently from other consultants.

A para-medical worker who found herself in the middle of the vortex recalled that Dr Higgs had been urged to slow down both by the hospital management, which tried to impose administrative controls on her work, and by colleagues who shared her project. 'I tried to persuade her to stop for a bit, but she just quietly said, "I can't." I got the impression that her perception was that we were powerless and therefore we weren't going to be helpful. She was very clear about who had power.'

It wasn't only the powerless who were overridden, however. Dr Jane Wynne had hardly met Dr Higgs, and was called in to serve on an independent second-opinion panel set up in Cleveland during the crisis to monitor sexual abuse diagnoses from Middlesbrough General. She thus got to know her a little better during the May–June crisis. She urged Dr Higgs to bide her time. She too was ignored.

Social Services Director Mike Bishop called Dr Higgs in on 1 June to defend her diagnosis, which she did, but she would not bow to the department's pressure to slow down the rate of referral to social services, who were faced with a demand for care which existing guidelines – based on child neglect, torture and battery rather than sexual abuse – were inadequate to deal with.

To all of them, and to the inquiry itself when counsel pressed her hard about whether she heard the cautionary voices, her defence was disarming: 'What you are faced with is the patient or the child in front of you, and you have to give an opinion and make a decision about the problem as it presents itself to you.'

Dr Higgs' colleagues' advice to slow down was not a denial of her diagnosis; it was more a counsel of *political* caution in the absence of adequate material as well as ideological resources to *plan* protection. It was a demand that Dr Higgs have the courage to stay silent, to watch and wait, when what that might mean was perhaps nothing less than returning a child to a rape situation.

Of course it was not only the volume but the diagnosis itself. It was new to many of her colleagues, including Dr Wyatt, who quickly became converted once he'd seen it, and began diagnosing it himself. This is less surprising than it seems – anal dilatation is apparently an arresting sign, and once you've seen it you can't miss it. It seems rather like an orgasm, or a sneeze, or a duck-billed platypus – there's nothing else quite like it.

Dr Higgs felt confident of the diagnosis because it was affirmed in the *only* available academic research – the paper by Dr Wynne and Dr Hobbs. The only challenge was Dr Raine Roberts' letter in the *Lancet*, which covered older children than those cared for by Drs Wynne and Hobbs, and it contained no detailed data. And contrary to the impression created by her interrogators during the inquiry, anal dilatation was a familiar diagnosis of buggery in all the forensic textbooks used by police surgeons – despite the claim by Dr Roberts and Dr Irvine, who held the minority belief, that it was an irrelevant sign and could appear in 'normal' bottoms.

Dr Higgs under siege

By mid-June Dr Higgs was under siege. It was then that Community Health Council (CHC) secretary John Urch, who saw the CHC as the 'conscience' of the health authority, approached the police and social services to voice his concern. He was told that the chief constable had issued instructions to divisional commanders that 'unsubstantiated evidence from Dr Marietta Higgs will not be a matter for investigation'. He turned to social services in a bid to stop them taking care orders – enabling the county council to remove children from at-risk situations – because he believed that 'here were two paediatricians creating a situation which nobody felt they could do anything about stopping . . . It was like hellzapoppin land.' On behalf of the hospital's 'consumers' – presumably parents – he wanted it stopped. In mid-June he rang Dr Higgs. 'I suppose I was rude . . . but she never lost her temper, she did not raise her voice.'

She was both serene and modest – and she never made claims beyond what she knew. These qualities produced a resilience which impressed even Dr Higgs' critics during her week as a witness to the inquiry. But these same strengths seemed to drive her assailants to excess. 'I called her everything I could lay my tongue to really, in all sorts of ways, but the response was cool and calm,' Mr Urch told the inquiry. When asked what he expected her to do, he simply reiterated that she refused to co-operate. When asked what he would have done to protect children, he offered no strategy. He admitted that he was 'basic and aggressive. It is true, I was, but it was to produce some response from this cool, calm, unruffled lady; some response to show that she cared, that she understood, instead of this – as she sits now looking at me – it seems so unreal.' What exactly was unreal? A woman who would not bow to any amount of bullying?

Her critics gestured towards the need to do something about the scourge of sexual abuse, but none offered an alternative protection plan. Mr Urch lined the CHC up with the police, Middlesbrough MP Stuart Bell and the local vicar, the Rev Michael Wright to protect the 'community', by which he meant not children but parents. Most of his time during those early days of summer, he said, was spent processing complaints by aggrieved parents and pointing them in the direction of Rev Wright's Parents' Support Group.

John Urch echoed widespread anxiety when he criticised the conditions in which children in Cleveland were being taken into local authority care, but his critique was more than that. It was infused with disgust at the diagnosis itself. 'It seems wrong just to go ahead, touching bums, making a diagnosis, kids in care, bring the brothers and sisters in, fill wards up, ship some of them to North Tees because there was no room; and we had to plead with North Tees to give facilities in the gymnasium. They would have been better in prison.' And, he suggested, it was all Dr Higgs' fault.

Behind all this was a struggle for power and control. What Mr Urch wanted was 'proper managerial control of the consultants'. The campaign for accountability would no doubt have enjoyed resonance among many in the community who felt that their battered health service did not meet their needs. But the struggle for control had begun to be waged against the very paediatricians who had tried to defend and even to improve services for children *before* the crisis in May and June.

Empire-building was already on the tip of his tongue before Stuart Bell accused the paediatricians of just that in his speech on 29 July in the House of Commons. Dr Higgs, he added, had 'conspired and colluded' with Sue Richardson. Bell and Urch suggested that people were voting with their feet and boycotting paediatrics. But South Tees Health Authority figures showed that during the crisis, which received massive local coverage from May, there was no evidence that patients were absenting themselves. Parents, presumably mothers in the main, were still taking their children to Middlesbrough General. There was no marked increase in the number failing to keep appointments.

Nevertheless, by September, when both Dr Higgs and Dr Wyatt were on leave and attending the judicial inquiry, paediatricians' diagnosis of sexual abuse among children attending Middlesbrough General Hospital had completely ceased. Not a single child was referred by paediatrics to the hospital's special Children's Resource Centre. In 1988 Dr Higgs was transferred from Middlesbrough General to work in Tyneside, and although the usually irrepressible Dr Wyatt remained in his old post he was banned from handling any child abuse or sexual abuse work. Suspected sexual abuse cases were seen in the outpatients department, though these had usually been sent by social services, who continued to detect sexual abuse much more vigilantly than before the crisis. And some nurses continued to alert the paediatricians to children who worried them on the wards. But the paediatricians were paralysed, not only by the political mood, but also by the continuing problem of the police. According to one doctor in Middlesbrough General in 1988, 'It is very difficult to take cases anywhere. If the police don't get a confession from an alleged perpetrator then nothing happens. They interview the people involved and that's it. I know Marietta found the same attitude, it's not changed, it's just hardened. You feel quite helpless.'

Outpatient referrals		*Failures to attend*
May	790	181
June	1069	208
July	948	205

The gender factor

The community appeared to be represented by men: Stuart Bell, John Urch and the Rev Michael Wright. Their enemy: two women, Dr Higgs and Sue Richardson. What these masculine alliances disguised was the presence of men like Dr Wyatt, the more cautious Dr Peter Morrell, Social Services Director Mike Bishop, male social workers and members of the hospital management who lined up with these women. These men were represented not so much as allies, but as wimps and weaklings in the thrall of the unseemly strength of insubordinate women.

But the gender factor was salient to Cleveland. Dr Higgs appeared inaccessible to any kind of pressure. Her calm and her commitment seemed, in themselves legitimate grounds for criticism among these men. As it turned out, her stoicism in support of the diagnosis was not unfounded, but what seemed to enrage these men was not only that they thought she was wrong, and that current estimates of the incidence of child abuse was crazy, but that they could not *force* her to change her mind.

Although the allegations of conspiracy against Dr Higgs and Sue Richardson made by Stuart Bell in the House of Commons were dismissed by all except the police in the final submissions to the inquiry, there remained a sense of, if not conspiracy, a network, an underground of women like Marjorie Dunn, Dr Higgs and Sue Richardson. For the Rev Wright at least, they seemed to be a feminist mafia. Social Services Director Mike Bishop told the inquiry that he himself had not co-operated with Rev Wright because the priest 'could not keep his own emotions out of the situation'.

The reverend has strong views on women, and on feminism, which he believed was a powerful presence in the crisis. There was, Wright said, 'a strong element of evangelistic crusading coming across, in which the feeling was conveyed by people who are obviously women, many of them divorced or single parents, that families would be better off without fathers. That caused a great deal of anger. It may well have a lot to do with the fact that a lot of people involved are women. Certainly the line was being put across that families would be happier without fathers and this was laid at the door of feminism.'

Ironically, Dr Higgs remained implacably anti-feminist and disengaged from politics. 'I'm totally apolitical,' she'd say. Her confidence came not from the politics of child sexual abuse, nor a critique of the structures of social and personal power operating within and without the family system, but from her job.

Her life has moved between her home, with her own large family, and hospitals, with their children's wards. It was a dedicated but sheltered life. It was as if she was not afraid because she did not see the enemy. She hadn't counted the battalions ranged up against her, and consequently had not built up the necessary alliances to protect her project. She was a political ingenue. This made her brave, but it also made her morally militant rather than strategic. A friend of mine once asked, 'What is it with her, what does that Mona Lisa smile mean?' Perhaps there was no mystery, perhaps Marietta Higgs is exactly what she seemed to be – a strong, pleasant woman, rather more ready to smile than five grim days in the witness box allowed, sure of her skills and equally sure of her limits. Perhaps she protected herself from the calumny by staying within the boundaries of her professional obligations. There was, for example, no strategy to deal with children's silence, for diagnosis without disclosure. It was her job to diagnose and then help to heal hurt children. It was everyone else's job to do the rest. And when they couldn't she perhaps believed, as they say in *The Hitch-hikers Guide to the Galaxy*, that it was Someone Else's Problem.

Dr Higgs believed that she was right and she believed in the truth. Others, too, would ultimately believe in the truth. She understood that she was being treated in the same way that children had been treated – her truths were being denied. Like many abused children, she had no strategy for survival beyond her own strength.

If the disbelievers could not make her change her mind, neither could anyone else. For Dr Higgs' supporters the objective was different: they urged caution because they feared that Dr Higgs could protect neither the diagnosis, the children, nor ultimately herself from a calumny that might throw back the cause of child protection by a decade. Whether Cleveland does that entirely depends not on Marietta Higgs, for she was only doing her best, but on the kind of alliances that may be wrapped around abused children, personally and politically.

One of Dr Higgs' and Dr Wyatt's colleagues in Middlesbrough, Dr Peter Morrell, affirmed their diagnosis, but explained the difference between their approach and that of many others who adhere to the diagnosis and its implications. 'I never wanted to retreat from it, because sexual abuse is a major problem and the outlook for the abused child is so bad that you can't ignore it. I tried to support everything that happened here. My views are rather different, though. I wasn't as vigilant as they were. They are both strong paediatricians who vigorously seek it out. Whereas if I was faced with it, I'd make the diagnosis, but I wouldn't seek it out. I feel their approach is better. It probably does need seeking out. A lot of it won't come to light spontaneously, because there are a lot of secrets. The hospital management would have preferred it not to have arisen at all, to have it contained as before, not spoken about. They got a tremendous shock. I feel it's something that's been missed before – perhaps even ignored, not missed.

'But it is a heck of a thing to take on. It entails a lot of difficulties coping with the parents and the children, a lot of work, apart from the emotional thing. Once you've made the diagnosis you probably spend half a day contacting social services, talking to parents, then there's case conferences and court appearances. I see 100 children a week – so it's a heck of a workload. It's straightforward why people back off. It is much more difficult than child abuse, it's not easy for anyone. Once you've raised it, it is very difficult to back down. It's probably the last time you see the parents, it's very difficult to hold.'

Another colleague had more contradictory feelings. 'She [Dr Higgs] was finding the signs of abuse, she realised that it was her duty to report it, but she separated herself from the consequences. She had her area of responsibility, other people had theirs. Okay, you can't knock that. But she couldn't hold it. My anger is that she wouldn't listen, she had to *save* the children.'

One of Britain's widely respected child abuse therapists told Dr Higgs during a summer seminar in 1987, in the midst of the crisis, that she was doing just that, trying to save the children. 'You mustn't,' he said, 'you must wait, you shouldn't try to rescue.'

'I have to,' said Dr Higgs.

A colleague of Dr Higgs who listened to this exchange reckoned: 'That's the hardest bit. You can't knock it when you know the damage sexual abuse does. It was as if it was like immunisation, a medical matter. I think she thought the resources would be found – it is dreadful to say that she did it to get the resources, I don't believe that. But she did it without a real knowledge of the implications.'

Some of her colleagues decided not to urge caution because they felt, quite simply, that she could *not* do nothing. But while taking *moral* responsibility for the children, she was felt by some of her allies not to have taken professional responsibility for other colleagues equally committed to the children. And that meant planning a strategy for protection. As another child abuse specialist involved in some of the Cleveland cases put it, 'She tried to do the right thing the wrong way.'

Some colleagues urged her to be cautious, which would perhaps have meant not telling parents immediately of her suspicions of sexual abuse, avoiding early polarisation, monitoring children over time while alerting other agencies and considering appropriate forms of protection. Dr Higgs' honesty with parents was undoubtedly honourable, yet it often also polarised positions, with paediatricians in one corner and parents in the other, leaving little room for other professionals to encourage all parties gradually to face up to the implications of the diagnosis. Was it worthwhile, some wondered, to leave everyone in pieces without having the means to help them put themselves together again? Such an approach demands time and resources – and, therefore, money. It would, of course, have placed on the paediatricians a much greater burden than was felt by those who simply denied that sexual abuse was taking place. The disbelievers never had to take responsibility for abused children. Dr Higgs and her colleagues did.

Either way, Marietta Higgs had no control over her reputation. Much of the media positively incited hatred of her. Unusually, given the media's obsession with her persona, here was a mother of five children who were not pictured in the press. Indifferent to the family she had made for herself on its own doorstep, the *Daily Mail* went all the way to Australia to dig up her long-lost father, and ran a double-page spread on 30 January 1988 showing him as a down-and-out divorced by her mother when Marietta was a child. It was not lost on Dr Higgs that the press preferred to represent her as a solitary figure, a woman without relationships, without networks, without a neighbourhood. It became a familiar motif in the 1980s, the undomesticated working woman aloof from the world of the *real* woman, the family. Curiously, Marietta Higgs' world was, in some ways, a traditional woman's world – a world populated by children, her own and hundreds of others. None of this impinged on the character constructed by the media.

What was known about Marietta Higgs seemed either to generate empathy among many women who endorsed her courage and grieved for her in the wake of the witch hunt, or it confirmed a caricature of someone coldly crazy. A schoolteacher in a Newcastle comprehensive heard a pupil protest that 'That Dr Higgs is bent!' Her fate brings to mind Nathaniel Hawthorn's story, *The Scarlet Letter*, about Hester Prynne, a dignified young woman who gave birth to a daughter out of wedlock and was punished by her Salem community for the sin of sex. Her punishment was that she had to wear a large, scarlet letter A for Adultery across her bosom. Like Hester Prynne, Marietta Higgs, with her unimpeachable integrity, may for ever wear the mark of sex. Only this time she may wear a scarlet A for Abuse, for a society that refused to take responsibility for its own truths, and then blamed her when she did.

Doctors under scrutiny

Newspaper readers and television viewers who had not been privy to the discussion in the academic journals had the opportunity to hear the professionals defend their positions before public scrutiny when the inquiry began in October. The inquiry's brief was to examine arrangements for dealing with sexual abuse and its diagnosis. Anal dilatation was the focus of debate: at issue was its efficacy as a sign and the method of diagnosis. The impact of disbelief on the media's coverage of the Cleveland crisis was such that *The Times* on 3 August 1987 confidently suggested: 'Before the inquiry is over the anal dilatation diagnosis may have been largely discredited.' *The Times* was wrong. By the time the inquiry was over the diagnosis was largely vindicated. It was supported by a consensus among both paediatricians and police surgeons. Dr Roberts and Dr Irvine were almost alone in insisting that it was largely irrelevant. Indeed Dr Irvine changed his mind towards the end of the inquiry and admitted that it might be a useful sign.

The only specialist prepared to support Dr Roberts'

insistence on the sign's irrelevance was Dr Richard Heald, a surgeon practising in the southern English overspill town of Basingstoke, and specialising in coloproctology – the colon and rectum. He believed that the buggery of children was a *rare* (his emphasis) perversion which, he said, he'd hardly seen in his 20-odd years 'seeing all the abnormal anuses and rectums in a very average English district'. His message to the inquiry was that anal abuse of children was exceptionally rare 'in my part of the world anyway'. After talking it over with some of his colleagues, he concluded that, 'I find all of my colleagues feel much as I do: that they cannot believe that they could have missed over a lifetime of coloproctology practice something which was happening with the frequency that it is being alleged . . . it is highly improbable to us that infants and small children are being regularly buggered.'

He had, however, seen anal dilatation in his patients over the years, notably in women and children, 'but I had not really thought about it in a serious way until I began to read in the press the apparent significance that was being attached to what I had always thought was normal.' So, Dr Heald thought it was normal and could see 'no possible sexual abuse basis for that physical sign'. It was not that he had any clinical basis for thinking it either normal or abnormal, but he determinedly believed it to be normal because, simply, he did not believe that sexual abuse could have taken place. 'I am absolutely satisfied in my own judgement that they were clearly families in which the question of buggery was quite inconceivable.' Furthermore, he did not initially take the *Lancet* article by Drs Wynne and Hobbs very seriously until the Cleveland controversy, and then only 'because of the *terrible things which have happened to the relatives* of some of the children' (my emphasis). After being reminded of descriptions of the sign in the medical literature, he provided a clue to the difficulty many doctors were having in coming to terms with the dilatation diagnosis: 'I went through medical school and did quite well, and I never heard of this physical sign. Indeed, so did many others. It is not a physical sign I was ever taught at medical school. For most practitioners of medicine it is a new physical sign.'

Dr Heald's disbelief seemed to be rooted in the no doubt correct conviction that if the paediatricians were right then he and his colleagues had been wrong. However, his disbelief was founded on something more than professional pride: he suspected 'a sort of witchcraft hunt' for sexual abuse, and rightly reckoned that 'a physical sign to be valuable to a doctor has to have meaning'. If the sign implied sexual abuse then he for one was convinced that it would be proved to have no meaning – because it could not mean sexual abuse.

The Police Surgeons Association's evidence to the inquiry gave an unexpected, though qualified, endorsement to the diagnosis: anal dilatation was *significant*, and its appearance should give rise to '*strong suspicions*', it said. The association later took the extraordinary step of trying to amend its evidence to the inquiry, by removing the word *strong*. This was a result of some debate at the association's autumn symposium. Although the association would not abandon recognition of anal dilatation as a significant sign, this was regarded as a gesture towards Drs Roberts and Irvine. The association's evidence had been prepared by its honorary secretary, Dr Hugh De La Haye Davies, an affable Northamptonshire country doctor. He was proud of his county's collaboration with social services and child protection agencies as well as the local rape crisis centre. He had successfully negotiated with the latter a special rape suite in Northampton police station, accessible through a separate entrance. His readiness to negotiate distinguished him from Dr Roberts.

During the inquiry, what emerged as more controversial than the diagnosis was the method of examination itself. No paediatrician defended internal examination of the anus by doctors inserting their fingers. The police surgeons' tradition recommended internal examination, but even that depended on the doctors' discretion. How could the paediatricians be sure of dilatating anuses, Irvine and Roberts argued, if they didn't insert their fingers and *feel* the tone of the anal canal. The paediatricians replied that you didn't need to *feel* it, you needed to *see* it.

Mrs Justice Butler-Sloss pushed the point with Dr Roberts: 'It seems to be a fairly firm paediatric view that you would not have a digital examination. You would say, I take it, that no paediatrician could therefore give a proper diagnosis?'

'That is right, unless there were obvious signs of acute injury,' replied Dr Roberts. But the sign was associated with chronic, not acute, abuse. And in any case, her Manchester colleague Dr Frank Bamford, a prestigious Reader In Paediatrics, with whom she had performed several joint examinations, said he had never seen her do an internal.

Oh dear. Dr Roberts, the star witness for the 'disbelievers', was in trouble. More than fingers versus eyes was at stake. Police surgeons' claim to be the experts on sexual crime hung in the balance. Newcastle social services director Brian Roycroft reminded the inquiry that the detection of child abuse had quadrupled nationally over a five-year period, and the most striking increase had been found in a handful of disparate areas, among which 'only one feature seems to be in common: increased awareness and activity by the hospital-based paediatricians'.

In her evidence to the inquiry, Dr Roberts made a widely reported accusation that the Cleveland paediatricians had been guilty of 'outrageous sexual abuse' of children, that screaming infants had been held down during the examinations. It was one of the most memorable, and widely reported, moments in the inquiry. During cross-examination, however, Mrs Justice Butler-Sloss reminded Dr Roberts that this allegation had not been levelled by any parents. 'If that is not the case I will certainly withdraw it,' she told the judge. Nor had any nurses alleged it, said the judge. Mr Anthony Kirkwood, QC, representing the Official Solicitor and the children, also challenged her, and Dr Roberts parried: 'Perhaps you could ask the children.'

'Dr Roberts, we have,' he said.

Though her original accusation had been headlined by the media, her reluctant retraction was reported in only one paragraph at the bottom of one report in the *Guardian*.

Dr Roberts regarded anal dilatation as 'mostly' absent from the few diagnoses of anal abuse. In a series of 103 cases of sexual abuse confirmed by her in 1986, there were only eight cases in which anal abuse was alleged. Only four of them were confirmed and only three of them included anal dilatation as part of her diagnosis. This appeared to be a contradiction, however. Three-quarters of this albeit tiny sample did contain anal dilatation.

Dr Roberts, like Dr Irvine, also believed that anal dilatation could appear in 'normal' children, although neither offered any data to support the idea, and it found no support from any specialist other than Dr Heald. She admitted that she had conducted an experiment – which, she was reminded, some might regard as 'outrageous' abuse, too – on a child's buttocks to prove her point (although the anus did not dilate). And for his part, Dr Irvine, too, said he had been doing 'casual' research on some children, without the consent of the profession's ethics committee, or the children's parents. He had seen anal dilatation in his own general practice, but he knew the family concerned, and sexual abuse was unthinkable.

'I make no bones about it – this practice is highly improper,' said Mr Kirkwood.

Dr Roberts mobilised threadworms as her accomplice: they seemed to cause the 'greatest difficulty in diagnosis. Threadworms have been present in a number of Cleveland children who have been diagnosed as sexually abused without any other finding.' Threadworms were certainly regarded as an alternative explanation by solicitors initially involved in defending dissenting parents. This surprised several doctors, not least Dr Bamford. Around 20 per cent of children have them at any one time. These tiny creatures, like strands of cotton wool, travel through the body, coming out at night, often causing itchiness around the anus. They couldn't cause dilatation, he said, because that was caused by something big enough to rupture or stretch the sphincter muscles. Anal dilatation was a function of the dynamic between the sphincters in the anal canal, a symptom of sphincter solidarity under stress.

He then described the architecture of the anus. When the internal sphincter was weakened, it could be only briefly supported by its sister muscle. That was why a cursory sighting of a shut bum wasn't long enough. If the exhaustion of the external sphincter was not supplemented by the internal sphincter then what you got wasn't a dynamic canal with its locks and gates but a hole.

'If the internal sphincter muscle is damaged, and it can be damaged by stretching, then the external sphincter muscle is the only muscle which can close the bowel off adequately as you begin to inspect the anus. The problem is that the external sphincter muscle can only sustain a contraction for a relatively short period of time, and whilst the child may contract the muscle when you initially begin to examine him, because he cannot sustain the contraction, that muscle gradually relaxes and if the internal muscle has been stretched and is not working the anus gapes and you can see inside. It is quite clear that anal intercourse can stretch that muscle.' That was 'the whole essence of the sign'.

Dr Roberts also proved to be vulnerable on children's sexual anatomy. She attacked Dr Fraser's meticulous measurements of girls' hymens to discredit her assessment of abuse. Dr Fraser was wrong, she said, citing the eminent gynaecologist Sir John Dewhurst. No, the judge reminded her, Sir John had confirmed Dr Fraser's calculations. That left Dr Roberts, once again, in the wrong.

The politics of the orifice

The politics, as against the anatomy, of sexual abuse hardly featured in the inquiry. When it did, it was perhaps not surprisingly in the form of a challenge to Dr Wynne and her Leeds team from Simon Hawkesworth, QC, for the parents. In 1987 Dr Wynne and Dr Hobbs had written an article in the *Archives of Disease in Childhood*[1] which touched on the problem of power. It supported a passage in an article of mine that summer in the *New Statesman*,[2] which suggested that the professional conflict mirrored the political conflicts over child sexual abuse, with paediatricians appearing as the political allies of the powerless and the abused, the children, while the police surgeons were upholding traditional authority, the parents and the police. Drs Wynne and Hobbs' article went on to argue that 'it is as much these differences in philosophy that prevent us moving closer to Dr Roberts' view than merely the interpretation of the scientific material'. Asked at the inquiry how that philosophical difference affected the medical assessment, Dr Wynne explained: 'If you accept that child sexual abuse happens then you accept that there must be a lot of adults abusing, and it starts to say something about our society: who we are, the way we live, and the way we treat each other.'

Mr Hawkesworth complained that the *New Statesman* article made 'what can only be described as party political points' by arguing that Stuart Bell's crusade 'has synchronised with Thatcherism's resurrection of the besieged family'.

'At last,' murmured another woman journalist on the press benches at the inquiry, 'we're talking about the politics of it instead of days and days about anuses.'

'As you well know,' Dr Wynne said to Mr Hawkesworth, 'women have had a struggle to have equal rights in this country, and it seems to me that if women are the chattels of men, and children belong to families, then you have to wonder where the children are and where the children's rights are.' Strategies for helping not only children and mothers but also perpetrators raised political issues, because unless governments were persuaded that sexual abuse really happened on a wider scale than had been imagined, resources to help people would not be found 'and it will never get any better,' said Dr Wynne.

Inertia by successive governments and the institutional complicity in denying the scale of sexual abuse were not on the inquiry's agenda; neither were the political implications of the diagnostic controversy. Why did the emergence of a familiar diagnosis cause such a frisson of anger when it was applied to familial abuse?

The stability of the diagnosis during the last 100 years was registered in the plethora of forensic textbooks read by the judicial panel. The standard works on medical jurisprudence described anal dilatation, or gaping of the anal canal, as a significant sign when it was accompanied by a smooth surface around the anal edge, rather than the normal puckering, healed lacerations (fissures) and thickening of the skin produced by regular rubbing. These same characteristics were confirmed by one of the major protagonists on the side of aggrieved fathers in the Cleveland crisis, Harley Street's Dr David Paul. However, his work provided a prescient clue to the political panic which erupted in Cleveland. It was a panic about the naming of the guilty gender of the perpetrators – men. In a widely read 1977 article, he warned that 'because of the revolting nature of many of the acts alleged, and because of the very high degree of tension and hostility such allegations are bound to generate, it is beholden on the examining physician to exercise very great care'.[3]

But by 1986 his caution became more specific, showing a worry that the finger was pointing at men. Some professionals seemed to believe 'that the sexual abuser *must* always be a *male*'.[4] This seemed over the top when compared with a more representative view expressed by chief inspector Roy Downes, in charge of child abuse liaison in the Greater Manchester police, who told a conference in the city in 1988 that in the experience of the police, most abuse was carried out by men on girls.[5]

Perpetrators are typically male and abuse is an expression of a patriarchal sexual culture. But that truth, strongly lodged in the common sense of women, became political dynamite during the 1980s. It became the unsayable during the inquiry. It was almost as if a society which was finally being forced to confront child sexual abuse was at the same moment refusing to confront the character of the perpetrators and the sexual system which produced abuse. And although the modern women's movement, like its antecedents in the women's movements of the late nineteenth and early twentieth centuries, has been among those who brought sexual abuse out of the shadows, and has certainly focused on masculinity as a political problem, it was exiled from the national debate surrounding Cleveland.

What the obsession with anal dilatation did do, however, was *implicitly* put masculinity into the picture. For, as Dr Wynne explained to the inquiry, if there was an epidemic of sexual abuse, then there was also a mass of abusers. But while the inquiry looked at the *effects* on children's bodies, it did not look at the *cause*.

The work of the Leeds team destabilised the fixity of beliefs about the culprits as *strangers*. Their research confirmed the modern findings that children are typically abused by trusted men in their milieux. But their work also destabilised beliefs about sex. In the tradition of forensic pathology, buggery was associated with homosexuality and rape. And that tradition has provided a medical endorsement to the very creation of the modern concept of the homosexual. The hidden agenda of the inquiry was the prevalence of *buggery* and by implication, a challenge to the received wisdoms about the nature of masculinity. For if buggery was being perpetrated by fathers on their children, then that disturbed the belief that it was typically *homosexual*.

Clearly, the evidence of buggery of young children not only challenged the notion that it was, as one expert told the inquiry, 'a rare form of perversion', but it also challenged the assignment of buggery to the gay community. The significance of this is clarified by the history of the formation of modern ideas about sexual identity. Jeffrey Weeks' pioneering work on the history of homosexuality and the emergence of first a gay subculture and now a gay politics is instructive. In *Coming Out* (1977) he records that before the 1880s, the law on buggery was 'directed against a series of sexual acts, not a particular type of person. There was no concept of the homosexual in law, and homosexuality was regarded not as a particular type of person but as a potential of all sinful creatures.' But in 1885, during a period of intense regulation of sexualities, when the 'family had become the paradigm of a stable society', the Labouchere Amendment forged homosexual identity as a person rather than simply a practice, and homosexuality became, like prostitution, increasingly 'differentiated into "deviant" sub-cultures'. And yet Weeks notes that before 1885, 'the law against sodomy was a central aspect of the regulation of non-procreative sex and it was directed at men'.[6]

It seems that the canon of forensic pathology was part of the ideological material which assigned buggery to homosexual men. Although it has been assumed that homosexuality was proscribed because it was beyond the pale of reproductive sex, it may be that buggery became the crucial sign in an ideological formation which was designed to distinguish between two masculine orientations – to separate homosexuality from heterosexual masculinity. Homosexuality came to be aligned to femininity, as a predisposition to be penetrated rather than to penetrate. Heterosexual masculinity was nothing if *not* that. But of course homosexuality may involve both, and if it is seen in this way it remains typically masculine, something which heterosexual masculinity seems to have purged from its consciousness. Buggery is only one of the penetrating possibilities available to all men. Perhaps the

real goal in this ideological process was to solidify a defin-
ition of heterosexual masculinity as a refusal to yield, to be
entered, to receive, as a quest to separate itself from femininity, and from homosexuality, as the only sexual
orientation never to permit penetration – of itself. But the
presence of anal dilatation as a sign of buggery in child
sexual abuse has blurred that distinction, that enforcement of sexual difference *between men*.

Bizarrely, despite gay historiography and the prevalence
of anal acts in heterosexual sex, at the end of the decade
the judge continued to tell legal colleagues that 'anal
abuse' appears to be 'homosexual as far as I can see'. What
is at stake is how sexual ideologies produce and police
identities. If more boys than we know have been buggered,
why have they been unable to reveal this in retrospective
surveys, our only guide to prevalence? Why have they
buried it? Does the experience of penetration so disorien-
tate their sense of their masculinity, in a culture that
decrees penetration to be permissible only in heterosexuality, that it has to be banished from memory?

The evidence of buggery among children, though not
the major form of sexual abuse, challenges our beliefs
about patriarchal sexuality. What the Cleveland inquiry
would not contemplate when it considered the bodies of
children was what exactly they revealed about the behaviour of men.

Like it or not, suspicions of child sexual abuse, particularly the practices which featured in Cleveland, and which
were first revealed by the Leeds paediatricians, who
enjoyed a sympathetic reception in their professional association in 1988, concern acts which are illegal. The
penetration of children's anuses and vaginas is deemed
serious sexual crime. That is why the whole panoply of the
criminal law was brought to bear on the Cleveland

families. The implications for the family and for fathers in particular were exactly what affronted the disbelievers. *The Times'* columnist Barbara Amiel on 22 April 1988 noted Drs Wynne and Hobbs' assertion that it was this critique which formed the basis of the difference in philosophy between themselves and Dr Raine Roberts. 'What does this mean, I wondered,' wrote Amiel. 'How do you "philosophically" diagnose a disease or a criminal act? There is of course a constituency that does regard the family and police as class enemies and sees the issue of child abuse as the means to root such class enemies out.' There was no evidence during the Cleveland controversy of any such constituency, not least because sexual abuse has not been on the agenda of *class* politics. Sexual abuse is about sex. It is about gender and generations, desire and power.

Furthermore, sexual abuse has shifted throughout history as an issue which varies in its alignment to the right or to the left. The vigilant challenge to sexual abuse of children during the 1980s came not from a heterogeneous political alliance, but from a miscellany of people with diverse professional, personal and political interests, ranging from the police to social workers and feminists servicing the survivors of sexual crimes. Amiel's main target, Dr Jane Wynne, could at one and the same time defend the modern nuclear family as the best context for rearing children, as she did when she gave evidence to the public inquiry, and also acknowledge that she and her paediatric colleagues were obliged to protect not perpetrators but powerless children.

Undeniably, all the challengers confront the very problem that the disbelievers seem to deny: that the overwhelming majority of perpetrators are men. Amiel wrote that she would rather that 100 men go free than that one innocent man be punished. And no doubt so would the constituency she criticises. But she goes further than this: she says she would rather risk letting one guilty father escape than that 100 innocent parents be convicted. She misses the point. It is difficult, nay almost impossible, to convict any suspected perpetrator on much less than a confession, certainly unless there is formidable physical evidence and corroboration. Like most disbelievers she is mesmerised by the problem of parents, by whom she means fathers, and less concerned with the problem of how we protect children. Curiously, it was the challengers who raised the *problem* of sexual abuse, on behalf of women and children, and the disbelievers who raised the *politics*, on behalf of the patriarchs. As Amiel said at the end of her column, 'I have no doubt where my priorities lie.'

Notes

1 J. Wynne and C. Hobbs, 'Sexual Abuse in Children', *Archives of Disease in Childhood*, 1987.
2 Beatrix Campbell, 'The Hounding of Dr Higgs', *New Statesman*, London, 31 July 1987.
3 D. M. Paul, 'The Medical Examination of Sexual Offences Against Children', in *Medicine Science Law*, Vol. 17, No. 4, 1977.
4 D. M. Paul, 'What Really Did Happen to Baby Jane? – The Medical Aspects of Alleged Sexual Abuse of Children', in *Medicine Science Law*, Vol. 26, No. 2, 1986.
5 *Guardian*, 8 January 1988.
6 Jeffrey Weeks, *Sex, Politics and Society: The Regulation of Sexuality Since 1860*, London, 1981, p. 99.

SEX CRIME

The Politics of Policing

When the evidence is not evident

Sexual abuse presents the police with peculiar difficulties. Children's bodies aren't like automobiles with the assailant's fingerprints lingering on the wheel. The world of sexual abuse is quintessentially secret. It is the perfect crime, and disturbs the lore and language of detection. It usually leaves no fingerprints, no witnesses, no clues, no confessions. Detection of sexual abuse depends, more than any other crime, on the solitary testimony of the survivor, typically a woman or a child.

A society in which adults are estranged from the world of children, and often from their own childhood, tends to hear children's speech only as a foreign language, or as a lie. Women have been treated like children, as congenital fibbers, fakers and fantasisers.

But from the mid-1970s, the survivors have begun to alert political and police consciousness afresh to sexual crimes against women and children. Until that time we were policed by a force exiled from the experience of the victim. How could an overwhelmingly male police force – 90 per cent of police officers in Britain are men – take responsibility for the problem of men, and for the pain of women and children? Specialist policewomen's departments were abolished when equality legislation was implemented in 1975 – International Women's Year – and women were beginning to make more confident demands for the right to be serviced by their own sex. Before the decade was out, policewomen's specialist skills were being called up once again. The Home Office has been compelled to concede that women and children who have been sexually abused should have the right to be examined and interviewed by women – not because women are nicer than men, but because men are the abusers[1] and, apparently, because men didn't believe women.

The year 1983 was a turning point in British sexual politics. Roger Graef's tide-turning television documentary, in which Thames Valley detectives were revealed harassing a woman reporting that she'd been raped, provoked such controversy that the Home Office recommended that rape survivors should have the right to be examined by women. That year there were also two rape scandals which ignited protests against judicial policy. A young woman raped after hitching a lift was accused of 'culpable negligence' by the judge trying her case. The other case prompted the resignation of a government minister for failing to prosecute a rape even though the woman, who had scores of stitches to patch up her body after the attack, said she could identify her assailants.

Most crime is solved with the co-operation of the people. And yet many, if not most, sexual crimes against women and children are unreported because the people pessimistically expect little co-operation from the police. Yet most reported cases are 'cleared up' and still unprosecuted. Detection is always contingent. It depends on co-operation and a consensus about what matters, what is wrong, what hurts, what is visible and what is knowable.[2] Detection is above all about what is *evident* and what is *evidence*. But all this is dependent on political consciousness. Seeing is believing and yet evidence, like beauty, is in the eye of the beholder. If you don't believe children are sexually abused then you don't see the signs, even when they stare you in the face.

Sexual abuse, furthermore, has a centrifugal effect – the evidence scatters. The prosecution mode itself often throws away the jewel in the police crown – the confession. There is no incentive to confess. The police often find themselves with no bargaining power against a suspected perpetrator: he is not a criminal, he is only a man. Usually there is little to withstand the suspect's denial; it is only the child's word against his. It has always been a case of men's word against children's: men have been believed and children have been silenced.

As the new consciousness of sexual crime developed, new demands were made of the police and the state, not only for new procedures but also for a political realignment in relation to men. Sexual crime provokes a crisis of belief, of procedure and prosecution, and of course it challenges the way we think about the nature of crime and punishment. More than that, it demands the feminisation of the police and the judiciary. Sexual abuse of children now presents society with the ultimate crisis of patriarchy, when children refuse to protect their fathers by keeping their secrets.

We know the alternative – that children put their fathers' pain before their own and protect them, as they always have, with their silence. Until now all the institutions of the state and civil society have conspired to protect the men in general and fathers in particular and keep their secrets.

These are some of the elements of crisis which

confronted Cleveland constabulary in 1987. Had they been touched by the new pressure coming both from women victimised by men and from the Home Office over the past decade? Whose side were they on? And how did they resolve the crisis of evidence and detection which sexual abuse always provokes?

Throughout 1987, while public attention was constantly guided to the so-called 'controversial' protagonists – the doctors and social services – the Cleveland police were immunised from our attention. What protected the police from public calumny in the months after the crisis erupted, if it was not a patriarchal consensus? Cleveland constabulary quickly took the side of the fathers. They were critical actors in the drama, and their performance tells us much about that particular police force and about the nature of civil society in Cleveland and in many, if not most, British cities.

Although bobbies on the beat in Cleveland seem to have sustained fairly close collaboration with colleagues in other professions responsible for children, the police management seems to have seen negotiation with other agencies less as co-operation than as a challenge. During the summer of 1987 and throughout the judicial inquiry in the second half of the year, the police believed that Marietta Higgs and child abuse consultant Sue Richardson were the culprits: it seemed that these women were on trial while the police appeared in their familiar role as witnesses for the prosecution. Despite their singular achievement in the judicial inquiry of provoking explicit criticism from Mrs Justice Butler-Sloss, the assumption was that the police were not the problem. While the media trawled the personal lives of the 'accused' for incriminating evidence, the Cleveland police were spared investigation of the kind of force they were. But the crisis doesn't make sense without them. It was the police, after all, who first blew the whistle in the spring of 1987 and who unilaterally refused to co-operate with the paediatricians and social services.

Cleveland had an old-fashioned, heavy-duty force dominated by a prosecute-and-punish culture. It seemed inaccessible to the modernisation of police practices demanded by the victims of sexual crimes during the 1970s and 1980s. It had not shown itself ready to learn from the changing consciousness of crimes against women and children, nor had it familiarised itself with pioneering exercises in joint investigations by neighbouring forces in Northumbria and West Yorkshire, or in London's Metropolitan police. The Met had in 1984 embarked on a widely discussed review of the way police and social services interviewed children.[3] The pilot study was motivated by the belief that 'traditional methods of police interviewing . . . present obvious difficulties', not least because children's language usually did not stand up to the court's evidential demands and 'the child's vocabulary did not extend to recognised adult terminology'. The Met recognised the need to draw other agencies into the investigative process, and set up a pilot study in Bexley, a borough where rapport between police and social services was well established. Forces like Northumbria and Bexley represented the direction in which best police practice was moving. How did Cleveland match up?

It didn't. Faced with a stiff challenge to its resources and its procedures when Middlesbrough General Hospital escalated the rate of referral of suspected sexual abuse cases to the police and social services in spring 1987, Cleveland constabulary responded with masculine panic, then tantrums and a reliance on 'masculine intuition', all of which became palpable in the police evidence to the inquiry.

Their evidence argued that their difficulties began in the winter of 1986. The trouble 'always related back to the appointment of Mrs Richardson', Inspector Colin Makepeace told the inquiry. She had drawn together the relevant agencies to reform procedures for the management of suspected sexual abuse cases, and in that context she had complained about police absence from multi-disciplinary case conferences. She 'took objection to the fact that the police were not there', said Insp. Makepeace.

Although they were stung by this criticism, the police seemed ready to collaborate in the investigation of cases being referred to them early in 1987. But they were left reeling by a case in February, when they arrested the grandfather of a child who had disclosed sexual abuse. No evidence was brought against him after the child named her father – and the father was not interviewed. From then on they retreated. As Sue Richardson saw it, they apparently felt that the incident had left them with 'egg on their face'.

When the number of cases referred by the hospital for investigation increased dramatically from March, the police became increasingly unsettled by the doctors' diagnosis itself. In the past, a child's disclosure of abuse or the concern of other professionals usually initiated an investigation. But after Dr Higgs' appointment, 'that was turned on its face', said Insp. Makepeace.

Referrals were often coming 'uncorroborated' by children's disclosures of abuse or by a perpetrator's confession. In some of the early cases, the police seemed to try to extract information by heavy interrogation of both children and their parents, which only confirmed children's confusion – and silence. A classic case was reported by parents over a year after their nightmare began, in the *Sunday Times Magazine* on 29 May 1988. After a policewoman had failed to get any information from two children in hospital, a detective took over. 'He decided to try and browbeat a confession out of these two recalcitrant kids. He started on Mark, saying he was very angry with the children for wasting everyone's time. "We've got your dad down at the police station and unless you want to keep him there you'd better tell us what happened." When Mark still refused to admit that anything had happened, the detective shamelessly tried to manipulate the little boy.' It was as if the boy was a burglar.

Sue Richardson complained to the police after a detective reported to a case conference which was discussing the case of an 11-year-old boy who had been interrogated in March. The father, who was also under suspicion of sexually abusing his children, had apparently given permission for the police to push the boy as far as they felt was necessary. 'The boy was treated like a criminal, as a perpetrator,' she said. 'We had no place of safety orders in that case, so social services could not sit in on the interviews. It was so horrendous that when the detective came to a case conference there was total shock among the other professionals when he told us how he'd told the boy that he was a little so-and-so, that he'd pushed him until he cracked. He was quite open about what he'd done. Everybody else was stunned. There was silence.' That is, until Sue Richardson told the detective that she was horrified at the treatment of the child. 'I said it would probably prevent the child ever talking about what had happened to him.'

'The next day I received a *personal* telephone call from a detective inspector telling me that he didn't allow any criticism of his officers, that I had no place to criticise in a case conference, that the police were having quite enough trouble with that Higgs woman as it was, and that if I was going to start causing trouble as well he would "arrange for there to be repercussions".' Social services management never appear to have complained about this intimidation to the police management. Nor was the incident, recounted at the inquiry, seen by Mrs Justice Butler-Sloss as much more than a professional tiff.

Insp. Makepeace told the inquiry that one of his officers had responded to children's silences by reporting: 'You know I've been talking to a child who is really well aware of what we're talking about, and he's emphatic nobody's touched him.' As the rate of referrals from the hospital jumped in the spring, so did police officers' bullying become disbelief that sexual abuse had actually happened. Insp. Makepeace added that, 'The staff were coming back and saying, "This is just not right; we're not getting the right vibrations. My gut reaction is all against what is going on here."'

Experts in sexual abuse work are familiar with the burden that telling places on children – they are often reluctant to tell and, having told, often retract. It is part of the process of protecting the abuser, and of taking responsibility for the inevitably painful consequences of disclosure. Cleveland police seemed to take children's silence at its face value, unaware that they themselves might have compounded the child's crisis.

Police intuitions guided their brusque 'strike' at the beginning of May, when they refused to co-operate in the collection of evidence by banning photographs requested by Dr Higgs for use in the courts. Photographs are familiar sources of evidence in the courts, particularly to show injuries which disappear as they heal. Inspector Alan Walls explained to the inquiry: 'I told Dr Higgs that it was not our policy to photograph genitalia, only injuries which may be present in the immediate area . . . I told Dr Higgs that as far as my officers were concerned, I had instructed them not to take intimate photographs of persons of any age, only sites showing injuries, and that these would be taken at the request of the senior officer investigating a criminal offence.'

Bruises were a different matter, he said, because compared with 'an open anus' they were 'marks of violence'. Photographs of an open anus had no 'evidential value', he said. So, they had decided that an open anus was not a source of suspicion.

He was pressed by Robert Nelson, QC, representing Dr Higgs and Dr Wyatt: 'Signs of, for example, rupture to a hymen or reflex anal dilatation may well be evidential value to a court?'

'That is correct,' said Insp. Walls but, 'We have never been requested by any other person to take the photographs. I have never known a police surgeon request any photographs of the vagina or anus of any victim . . . without associated injuries . . . if there are scratches, bruises, anything physical that shows, the photographs will be taken.' Anal dilatation, if it was a sign, could be described verbally, he insisted.

Did he feel, asked Robert Nelson, QC, that he was 'in a position to decide, as opposed to the doctor dealing with the child and seeking to protect it, what constitutes an injury and what does not?'

Insp. Walls was adamant: 'There was no injury.'

Despite his assertion that instructions to take photographs had to come from the senior officer involved, he admitted when questioned by the judge that the police regularly visited the children's ward to photograph bruises and other injuries at the request of the paediatrician. 'So there was nothing unusual in Dr Higgs asking you to take a photograph?' she asked. 'That is correct,' said Insp.

Walls. He agreed with the judge when she then suggested that the police would not have thought it inappropriate to photograph 'bruises around the base of the penis' and that the real problem about the photographs 'was you did not think this particular request related to evidence of an injury'.

Police anxiety about the propriety of photographing children's genitals seemed to be powered by something more than prudence. Detective Superintendent John White explained that although the sheer volume of diagnoses and the weight of denial by fathers disturbed the police, the real problem was that they 'were embarrassed at what they saw. They were asked to put a camera up a child's backside and take a photograph of the anus. They did not like it. They could not see any evidential value in what they were doing.' And anyway, 'having looked at some of the photographs I would suggest, well I know for a fact, a jury would never get sight of them'.

The judge did not agree. 'It is not for the police photographer, is it, to decide whether something is to be evidence, where an expert asks?' Didn't the problem owe rather more to 'natural distaste?' she inquired.

The police embarrassed? Could brave men who inhabit the space between life and death, order and disorder, who are supposed to do their best to deal with the worst that their world throws at them not deal with their distaste? Suffering they might have been. Speechless perhaps. But embarrassed? Did this evidence matter so much that it had to be disavowed?

Or did the evidence speak the unsayable? Did it detonate a taboo which failed to forbid sexual abuse but only succeeded in keeping it a secret, keeping it outside *social* knowledge. Evidence is not neutral, nor does it fall from the sky: it has to be discovered. Detection is an ideological endeavour to make sense of a mystery. The police response to the available evidence in Cleveland does not make sense unless we try to work out why they – like many people – found it so impossible. If we take the police as the paradigm, then their problem was our collective difficulty, for the evidence not only challenged what they already knew as men, as social beings and as the police, but also what *could become known*. Their problems were multiplied by the protocols and criteria of judicial evidence which control what can be known. What was contested in Cleveland was what an aficionado of the thriller already knows, which is what the mystery might mean.

The evidence confronting the police thwarted their muscular denial that sexual abuse on the scale implied by the doctors' suspicions could be happening. Sexual abuse, whether revealed by children's testimonies or by the signs on their bodies, stands as an accusation against adults in general and men in particular. For the police there is a particular problem: as a praetorian guard of masculinity, sexual abuse faces them with an accusation against their own gender. Police and judicial mastery over evidence has for over a century enabled them to banish the sexual experiences of women and children. Was that mastery threatened in Cleveland?

The crisis was dramatised in Cleveland constabulary's purge of the photographs. We attach to photographs a kind of truth, but in Cleveland the dispute between the doctors and the police over the photographs revealed the way they represent diverse truths for conflicting interests. For the doctors, the photographs were taken within the conventions of forensic evidence. They were literally faceless anatomies displayed in maximum light, designed to preserve the evidence from its own death in the process of healing. In the context of the controversy over the diagnosis itself, the photographs preserved the power of truth, a power that the doctors no longer possessed. Preservation of the evidence became vital to Dr Higgs not only because of the tendency of anal dilatation to disappear but also because she was no longer believed; her verbal testimony about the 'speaking' sign was already in jeopardy. She needed something more than herself to support the diagnosis.

In a way, however, these apprehensive policemen provided clues to the depths of disturbance created by the diagnosis. Inspectors Makepeace and Walls were right, even in their incoherence, to draw the distinction between the genital signs Dr Higgs showed them and injury. Bruises or scars, rightly or wrongly, are read as simple, stable evidence of victimisation which, as we gaze at them, always recruit our sympathy for the victim and not the culprit.

But anal dilatation and abused vulvas and vaginas present signs of a different order of pain than, for example, bashed bones or rogue blood cells. They are glimpses of a *sexual relationship* which are disturbing both because they suggest the sexuality of children, and because they reveal how children take responsibility for relationships thrust upon them. They challenge the notion of childhood as asexual, precisely because they reveal children's *participation*, albeit under duress. They were more than victims, these Cleveland children; their bodies revealed active strategies for survival, which implicated them in the crime. And so they became exemplars of the precise cruelty of sexual crime: survival demands co-operation. Their bodies showed how they were forced to *receive* objects forced upon them, or rather into them, because they could not *refuse* them and there was nothing and no one around to rescue them from this responsibility. In the absence of any message from the child beyond its own body, in the absence of any sexual posture other than proneness, in the absence of any look of either collaboration or resistance, the sores, swellings, bruises and openings spoke the pain of the child's participation.

The photographs also dramatised the dilemmas surrounding sexual abuse precisely because they were photographs. As Roland Barthes has shown in his essay on the press photo, 'The Photographic Message', in *Image-Media-Text*, the photograph does not just speak the truth; it is the product of its context, and meanings are carried to it by the photographer, the media and the reader.[4] We know that for the doctors, the photographs were taken according to evidential conventions to support their diagnosis. But what did they mean to the police? If not evidence, then what? Here were photographs of sexual anatomies, and it is worth wondering how far their features – anuses and vulvas, prone, open, available to our gaze and to our fantasies – crossed the boundaries between 'evidence' and 'pornography'. Both categories are, after all, about a sexual relationship. If pornography places the viewer in the position of the 'lover',[5] then who are we when we gaze at the bodies of sexually abused children? These forensic photographs face the viewer – the police, paediatrician and the public alike – with a challenge: with whom will she/he identify?

The evidential photograph, like a pin-up, positions the viewer, but where the pin-up is intended to excite the viewer's sexuality by revealing the sexuality of the subject *for him*,[6] the photograph is supposed to suppress the sexuality of the viewer while exposing the sexuality of a victim. But how can it? Our eyes and our experience travel the contours of these bald pictures just as they would the painting of the nude or the pin-up. Where the pin-up exists for men's pleasure, what does the evidential photograph of the victim excite? Pain? Or pleasure, too? We are thrown into confusion, for what are we supposed to feel? And are we in control of what we feel? In the pin-up, the body before us is, of course, not the subject but the object because we, the viewers, are the subjects: we are in possession of what is seen. But what is the body of the child in the evidential picture saying to us? It jolts the viewer because the child is bereft of its environment, its toys, its potty, its teddy, its friends, its parents, the domesticity (not the assumed asexuality) that defines the context of childhood. The effect of the banishment of all the banal bits and pieces that fill the child's universe is compounded by another absence – the rest of the child's body, its fingers and its face. The child is not playing with itself, and so what we do not see is the child's sexuality as existing in and for itself. The picture invites us into the shocking realisation that the child has been sexualised because it is an object. In the pin-up the woman is made an object for the male spectator because she is sexual, but in both genres, the subjectivity of the child and the woman alike is denied by the *presence* of the *absence* – the viewer or, in this context, the abuser.

The evidential photographs of abused anuses and vulvas are more than painful – and that they are: they are troubling. They are sexual because they are defined not just by the child's body but by the invisible presence of the perpetrator. They are difficult pictures to see because what they show is not only a body but a relationship. They may cause you grief or they may work on your fantasies, but either way, you have to work out who you are as you watch, if you are to know what to think.

And so we can sympathise with the problem of any police force when faced with photographic evidence, and can ask ourselves where does the sense of propriety come from in police culture? Is it respect for children's modesty? Is it a refusal to believe that men like themselves could fuck children? Is it a reaction to repressed desire? Or is it a mark of the pain of their own past, the unspoken secret of their own childhood?

A crisis of detection

Usually the police would expect to proceed from a disclosure or familiar suspicions voiced by other professionals in cases of sexual abuse. The scale of the diagnosis in Cleveland, and then the diagnosis itself, presented the police with investigative complexities for which they were not equipped. What was at stake for the police was both a crisis of belief and a crisis in the very practice of detection. And so, in May and June, when *more* evidence was needed by the police, they sought *less* to save themselves from public failure in the one task that was uniquely their own: detection. Already detectives had been left with 'egg on their face', and so instead of refining their relationship with other professionals, perhaps even subordinating prosecution to protection of children in the absence of a prosecution, they set about establishing not guilt but innocence.

Deputy Chief Constable Jack Ord was asked at the inquiry whether the police insisted on calling in a second opinion 'in cases where there was no realistic hope of a prosecution, whatever happened'. He revealed that the police not only wanted to close files but, in the absence of establishing guilt, also wanted to prove innocence. 'It is proper, surely, first of all to see if the allegation is proper and has a sound base. If you do not do that, then you are left with this allegation hanging in the air, with all the effects that has on a variety of people.' He went further, however: the purpose was less part of the quest for proof of the suspicion than a quest to establish innocence. 'Surely we have an obligation not only to secure a prosecution but to establish innocence if you are innocent.'

For the police, Dr Irvine was instrumental in their desire to exonerate suspects. They so strongly disbelieved the diagnosis that they needed Dr Irvine not to confirm the diagnosis but to dismiss it. Where other police authorities have adopted a flexible relationship with both paediatricians and police surgeons, and where some authorities have relied increasingly on paediatricians to provide medical evidence, Cleveland constabulary sought second opinions that disavowed the diagnosis in principle.

That was why they became obsessed with the need to write the presence of the police surgeon into the multidisciplinary guidelines over which there had been so much wrangling in previous years. They saw the suggestion by social services that a paediatrician's diagnosis might suffice as a direct attempt to dispense with the doctor they trusted, Dr Irvine. And so, for the police, the 28 May meeting to finalise the guidelines was the crunch. What for social services was an attempt to specify that the police would act on an abuse diagnosis by any appropriate doctor was seen as an attempt to dismiss their man. What they were doing 'was taking away from me one of my instruments of investigation', said Insp. Makepeace at the inquiry. But Dr Irvine's hostility to the diagnosis was such that he could often be relied upon to take away the need for any investigation by the police.

The day after the 28 May debacle, which had ended without any resolution of the conflict over the relevance of the police surgeon, the police decided that Dr Higgs' diagnosis should be treated with caution and corroboration should be sought *before* taking action.

Det. Supt. White offered the inquiry several poignant vignettes of police pessimism about prosecution. In one case, after a long interrogation of a suspect which produced no admission, Det. Supt. White reckoned, 'It makes you wonder if there was any point. Nothing had arisen, nothing that could be put to the man that, I would suggest, he did not know about already. There was an allegation by Dr Higgs that the child had been sexually abused. Having said that, where did we go on that?' Detection, it seemed, depended on confession.

In another case, a three-year-old child showed physical signs that she may have been abused. There was 'partial disclosure' that 'daddy made it sore'. Det. Supt. White explained: 'The child had been in the swimming baths and would, I think, be naturally dried down by the father, which is what was virtually being said. The child at no stage made an allegation, and maybe never would have at that age, that it had been abused by anyone.' The child had vaginal infection as well as soreness, and several other professionals believed they had some form of supporting evidence.

Dept. Supt. White agreed that in this case there had been an allegation by the child that her father had touched her vagina. In fact, two of this man's children complained of being sore. A foster mother looking after the children when they were taken into care reported that one child's behaviour was 'inappropriately sexual' for her age: 'I have fostered children for the past 25 years and have never seen children do this before,' she said. Det. Supt. White told the inquiry that such behaviour 'would be an indication that something needed investigating, yes. I think then we have got to go on to see what the father's explanation is, which appears to be quite an innocent one.'

Another paediatrician at Middlesbrough General had looked at the children and found not only a sore and red vagina in one of them, but also a dilated hymen and a bruise on the inside of the right thigh. Yes, said Det. Supt. White, 'that is another factor that would have to be taken into consideration'.

The evidence mounted up. Health visitor Marjorie Dunn had reported that swabs taken from the vagina showed signs of a sexually transmitted disease. Det. Supt. White told the inquiry that he regarded this as something that could be explained by either 'an innocent cause' or a 'suspicious cause'. But at a case conference on 6 August the police reported 'No further police action. This inquiry be filed.'

Once again the vigilant voice of Mrs Justice Butler-Sloss intervened. If the police had come to their conclusion *before* the case conference, what would happen if more suspicions were brought forward? Would the police reopen the file or leave it closed, she wondered. It seemed that if the police didn't *control* the process of investigation, and if the process didn't move toward prosecution and punishment, then they had no stake in staying involved to support other agencies in protecting the child.

The police had no doubt felt humiliated by their own failure as detectives, and their difficulties and their marginalisation were compounded by the chaos at Middlesbrough General Hospital which rendered Dr Higgs and Dr Wyatt even more inaccessible. It seemed that either they closed the file on Dr Higgs, or she closed the file on them, by delaying tactics. It sometimes took weeks to get an evidential statement from her.

Nothing if not consistent, they went into the 28 May meeting called by Sue Richardson to finalise new guidelines for sexual abuse investigations not to negotiate but to take control. Senior officers rallied to defend the police corner even though, as they revealed to the inquiry, they had not followed the rows that preceded the meeting.

Jack Ord, the constabulary's second in command, said he hadn't known of police anxiety about the rate of referrals before the meeting. But he went anyway, to back up the police position, whatever that was. It was all about corporate solidarity. Ord's apparent innocence of the issues showed a management aloof from its own staff and the community at large.

All this was contrary to the tone of the Bexley pilot study – a salient exercise which had struggled through many of the same crises which were to paralyse Cleveland. Indeed, the study arose from the police conclusion that 'the police service should not deal with the very complex issues alone'. There would be 'pockets of avid support and pockets of scepticism, if not outright disagreement', and that was to be expected, concluded the Bexley Report,[7] but autonomous agencies should sort out amongst themselves which of their functions 'take precedence'. The key word was flexibility. 'Current police policy appears to allow for very little discretion for a flexible approach in determining and deciding, through a process of consultation, the most appropriate time for initiating an investigation,' it said.

The open hostilities in Cleveland between social services and the police became a war of the sexes, exemplified in the language used to describe the women whom police managers were up against. 'What was worrying was the obvious lack of objectivity on the part of Mrs Richardson,' Insp. Makepeace told the inquiry. During the 28 May meeting, 'She openly supported Dr Higgs 100 per cent . . . Dr Higgs gave me the impression of being besotted with her own convictions . . . There was a definite sense of the evangelical present in Dr Higgs' attitude, and without a

doubt Mrs Richardson is a convert and ardent follower . . .
the oracle and fountain of all knowledge on child abuse
who is never wrong. It would seem that Dr Higgs, supported by Mrs Richardson, are out to serve their own
interests . . . If the conclusions of Dr Higgs and associates
are correct then we are going to require a considerable
increase in resources to handle everything they are throwing at us.'

He agreed that throughout the row that day Dr Higgs
'sat quite quietly, quite firmly'. Insp. Makepeace regarded
Dr Irvine as 'one of the best police surgeons ever' and was
keen to explain that if the doctor ended up shouting at Dr
Higgs it did not mean he was out of control. 'It is
extremely difficult with Dr Irvine . . . because Dr Irvine
talks at volume 10 normally, if you understand what I
mean, so if I say he lost his cool, he was a bit louder than
usual. But I would not like to give the impression that Dr
Irvine lost all sense of control.'

The following day the police walked out of any alliance
against sexual abuse. Police management imposed a ban
on officers attending further meetings with social services.
This meant they boycotted a determining meeting on 1
June which completed the long-awaited guidelines.

This rather shocked the judge: 'To break off dialogue
does seem very sad, if I may put it like that,' she told Det.
Supt. White, who admitted that, with hindsight, to have
attended the meeting 'would have given us the opportunity
as well to explain to the whole committee what had gone
on, and we missed the opportunity'.

The judge wondered 'how were social services to cope if
the police refused to attend?'

'Madam, looking back I wish that we had gone because,
as I say, it would have given us a platform to express our
concern at the meeting of the 28th. We did not.'

Mrs Justice Butler-Sloss pressed on. 'Not only a platform. I am looking a little further than that. If you don't mind me saying, Superintendent, you are looking at it at the moment entirely from the police point of view. You do not live in a world which is peopled exclusively by police officers . . . Ought not the police to look to see the effect of their actions on other organisations with whom in the past, the present and the future they have to work?'

'There was no common ground,' said Det. Supt. White.

'Is it not your job to look for it? . . . It would be tragic if you ever let that happen again,' replied the judge.

After the 28 May collision, the Director of Social Services immediately advised staff in a memorandum to manage their cases and act upon Dr Higgs' diagnosis. The police were instructed in a memorandum from Jack Ord not to act on an uncorroborated diagnosis. But isn't the police function exactly that: to find corroboration?

'Was that not bound to clash with social workers in succeeding weeks?' asked Mrs Justice Butler-Sloss.

'Yes.'

'What depresses me is why you did not perhaps let each other know what were the guidelines of each discipline pending an arrangement to try to come to an accommodation,' she lamented. 'It was bound to cause a clash with social workers and the police . . . the result was that there was a clash on every possible occasion . . . there was a problem about communication, Mr Ord . . . You do not live in a vacuum . . . When your superintendent issues a memorandum of some importance which queries the competence of a paediatrician to diagnose on a particular subject, where you must know – at a lower level, at least – that social workers faced with such a diagnosis would be obliged to act, there were bound to be clashes . . . The fail-

ure of you to tell them and of them to tell you the guidelines upon which you were each acting was going to add to
that.'

'The point I am making is that the problem emanating
from one memorandum was much more grave and significant than from the other,' Ord argued.

He was also challenged by Mrs Justice Butler-Sloss over
the wisdom of the public statement he issued a month
later, accusing Sue Richardson of abandoning agreed
guidelines. Why had he assumed that they had ever been
agreed when the whole problem was that they had not, the
judge wanted to know.

The police were later to accuse social services of
reneging on procedures agreed by the county's Joint
Child Abuse Committee (JCAC) by being prepared to
dispense with the police surgeon, but Ord admitted
under pressure from the judge that negotiations with the
JCAC were 'incomplete' – the guidelines had not been
finally agreed. The trouble was that although police officers operationally involved with other agencies on sexual
abuse work had seemed ready to agree to joint investigations, police management were not, and had blocked
any deal for that reason. In 1985 the police management rejected the new joint approach emerging on the
Area Review Committee. In 1986 it intervened over the
heads of operational officers involved and again repudiated joint investigations, and in 1987 it stalled any
agreement by reiterating police primacy and autonomy –
contrary to the conclusions of the Home Office pilot in
Bexley. Nevertheless, Jack Ord insisted that the constabulary's public condemnation of social services was
correct.

The judge thought otherwise: 'As I understand it,
through the year 1987 the JCAC had never come to

agreement on any of the disputed matters . . . I do not think there was any agreement at all throughout 1987 . . . They had not approved the guidelines, Mr Ord.'

'No, they had not . . . The wording is not sufficiently precise,' conceded Mr Ord.

But that was not enough for the judge. 'I think it absolutely wrong.'

'It is wrong,' said Mr Ord.

Even that wasn't good enough: 'But that is not quite right; it is completely wrong because there was no agreement between the agencies and disciplines which had taken a great deal of time and trouble,' said Mrs Justice Butler-Sloss.

That conflict between the other child protection professionals and the police management defined their subsequent strategy. Having decided that social services were to blame, the police made a public statement at the end of June, attacking social services. This was done without informing social services and after snubbing their suggestion that they and the police make a joint fence-mending statement to the press. Mr Ord became ever-more belligerent.

'Quite frankly I think the suggestion was silly in the extreme,' he told the inquiry.

The judge was not impressed. 'Would it not have been a good idea to have taken on board the suggestion? . . . You turned it down out of hand.'

'Yes,' replied Mr Ord.

The press release on 29 June was the first public intervention by the police. It came only hours after Stuart Bell, MP, told them what he would be saying in his dramatic speech in the House of Commons that afternoon. Mr Bell read out his diatribe to the police management before making the speech and later that day the police issued their own, echoing his allegations against social services and the paediatricians.

Policing and the community

Just what kind of force policed Cleveland? 'They're a dreadful force,' moaned a seasoned police manager in another force.

Cleveland constabulary was conservative, given to prosecution rather than contemplation, and relatively uninspired by Home Office initiatives when they concerned *women and children*. Since 1983 the Home Office has encouraged police forces throughout the country to make special suites staffed by women officers available to the victims of sexual crimes. But the police have a problem: in every year since the abolition of separate policewomen's departments in 1975, a lower proportion of women than men have been promoted.[8] This has undermined the ability of the police to make suitably senior women officers available to deal with serious crime, including sexual crimes. Cleveland has even fewer women than the low national average: 8 per cent, compared with 10 per cent nationally. 'It's a very male, reactionary force,' said Councillor Bob Pitt, the scourge of Cleveland's police committee.

The force was secretive and insecure in its response to any challenge. Child sexual abuse clearly wasn't the first. It was preceded by some years of coldness between the police, probation and social services. 'There hasn't been inter-departmental co-operation for a long time,' said one professional familiar with all three. 'Social services–police co-operation has been floundering for years. The police attitude is, yes, we'll think about it, but we want to talk about Neighbourhood Watch, get the police into the schools. Our main drive is getting bobbies back on the beat, and we'll make a media issue out of violence in the centre of town until the politicians realise what we want is lots of bobbies sorting out the lads.'

The constabulary's attitude revealed a wider crisis in Cleveland's civil society. Conservative and patriarchal, there was little in society to make the police change. However, when the police were confronted by the agents of modernisation, and more importantly the feminisation of the state's institutions, they reacted with bombast and belligerence. Many police forces in the 1970s modernised their treatment, for example, of women battered in their own homes. But a study for Cleveland Refuge and Aid for Women and Children published in 1984, and based on evidence over a five-year period, reported that every woman interviewed who 'approached the police needing protection and accommodation encountered obstacles in receiving help from them'.[9] In the winter of 1986 the Home Office sent to all police force areas Circular 69/86, *Violence Against Women*, for circulation among the police and then social services and housing departments. It was not distributed by the Cleveland police. Instead it appeared six months later among the appendices to the minutes of an obscure little committee concerned with budgets for spending on police buildings. The county's police authority told the constabulary in 1987 to consult GPs, the rape crisis centre, the battered women's refuge and other relevant voluntary organisations on the plans. It didn't. The constabulary was reminded in February 1988 by the police committee, and again it did not consult the community. But in April the constabulary reported that it had consulted a doctor – Dr Irvine. Again in April, the constabulary was instructed to explain why it had not complied with the request to consult. Finally, it did: the rape crisis centre says it received the invitation to discuss plans two days before the proposed meeting, and the battered women's refuge says the invitation arrived a week after the meeting.

'Male-dominated committees shouldn't be making decisions on facilities for women without consulting them,' commented Councillor Pitt. 'They stuck up two fingers to the consultation decision and they treat people with contempt. It's a siege mentality.' Finding themselves with a once-in-a-lifetime luxury – the opportunity to make history – the constabulary decided to stick with its patriarchal past.

But if sex crime didn't animate Cleveland constabulary, then 'real' crime did. Chief Constable Christopher Payne chaired the Association of Chief Police Officers' working party which drew up a secret manual after the 1981 riots in London, Liverpool and Bristol, which proposed police training in paramilitary operations. That manual was used to plan the police ambush of striking miners at the now-notorious Orgreave picket in 1984.

In the early 1980s, when the Home Office was encouraging the police to reduce the proportion of young offenders confined to custody, Cleveland police were prosecuting a higher proportion of juveniles than any other force in the country. This was less an expression of vigilance and detection than a prosecution culture in the police force. According to research by John Macmillan at Teesside Polytechnic, between 1982 and 1984 Cleveland cautioned (an alternative to prosecution) the lowest proportion of boys of all police force areas in England, although by 1985, under pressure from both local social services and from the Home Office, they were in line with the national average. Even after 1984, Cleveland's courts were still using custodial sentences to a greater extent than elsewhere.

Cleveland constabulary's hard reputation was reinforced in 1982 when a local fish merchant won 'exemplary damages' against the force after being beaten up in police cells. Judge Myrella Cohen accused the police of lying and a cover-up. No officers were disciplined. A clue to the political climate in which the force operated in the 1980s was the refusal of the compliant Labour-controlled police committee to seek an independent inquiry.

That year the committee showed even greater loyalty to the constabulary in the wake of massive local media coverage of a leaked internal inquiry into allegations of corruption in the force by a former senior officer. Chief Constable Payne sought and secured an injunction banning media reports on the allegations. The leak tormented both the police and the police committee, which voted in December of that year to fingerprint *itself* to find the mole. Its zcal was thwarted only because the forensic laboratory would not authorise the exercise.

Secrecy was no stranger to the police committee – it had had the habit of keeping two sets of minutes: when a sensitive matter was being discussed it often confined them to 'confidentiality' and kept the records out of sight of elected members of the council.

What we are left with is an impression of a constabulary ill prepared for its role in a cultural revolution. When faced with the crisis over child sexual abuse, it fled first of all from the evidence – suspicious signs on the bodies of children. Then, having spurned the *forensic* evidence, the Cleveland police mobilised *political* disbelief in the implied scale of sexual abuse. They were thrown back on a conservative common sense, untouched by the new political consciousness of the 1970s and 1980s. They failed, too, despite Home Office encouragement, to consult the experience of their colleagues in other constabularies. The *evidence* before them implied an *epidemic*. Disbelief in both restored their 'masculine intuition'. It reaffirmed their corporate identity against its challengers.

The language of their critique of Sue Richardson and Dr Higgs was entirely gendered: rationality versus unreason; stubborn, obsessed, besotted, neurotic, knowing witches versus the common-sensical bobby, sanguine, sensible, seeking reconciliation. All these terms, of course, described the opposite: the women were sombre, rational, calm. And what was perhaps unforgivable, they *knew more* than their police protagonists. The women just sat there while bombastic men threw tantrums and threatened. To no avail. Whether these women were right or wrong, they were inaccessible to any form of pressure. For that, too, they could not be forgiven. They were brushed with 'feminism' – not as a description but as an accusation. In the face of all that the police celebrated their own instincts and intuitions, those gendered terms usually thrown at women, but reserved this time for a militaristic but weak management, as a mark of their common sense.

A local youth worker closely involved with both social services and the police described the problem thus: 'It's about control and containment: "Let's not think about it, just do it."' He believed that disposition permeated not only the police, 'but the whole of our political culture here in Cleveland: it is inert, monolithic and based on common-sense conservatism. It's materialistic, patriarchal and its reaction is: if we don't understand it let's suppress it, or rather let's pretend it's not there.'

That seems to have guided the police through the storms of 1987. Their approach to public relations was to use PR, in Jack Ord's words, as a platform. It was for propaganda rather than consultation with the community.

Cleveland constabulary, however, might have ridden the

crisis had it learned from the sex-crime specialists setting up child protection units in other forces and the delicate diplomacy which produced them, in spite of entrenched opposition to the very notion of specialism endemic in the British police.

Reforming the investigators

The reformation began with rape. The first of Britain's 60 or so rape crisis centres was set up in London in 1976 when official police policy was to let a woman 'make her statement and then drive a coach and horses through it'.[10] A senior policewoman working on sexual crimes recalls how the police mind has changed during her 20-year career:

'The received wisdom about rape used to be: "It's rubbish, it's always rubbish." When you go to CID (Criminal Investigations Department) as a woman police constable, you are on your mettle to get sufficient Brownie points, and because you are a woman you interview rape victims, and you come out of those interviews with a *retraction*. That proves what a good detective you are. If you come out with a statement saying it happened, then the reaction would be: "Let's get somebody in who can do a proper job." I don't want to be a feminist, but some of the things that go on, honest to god . . .'

Northumbrian alliances

Cleveland's neighbouring force, Northumbria, invites scrutiny because it embarked on an unusual, perhaps unprecedented, alliance not only with child protection agencies but also with political movements organising against sexual oppression. The process began in 1977 when Tyneside Rape Crisis Centre (TRCC) wrote asking the police for talks. The request went to Superintendent Rhona Cross, now retired, who became a senior community development staffer in 1975. She had already been involved in reforming child abuse procedures, and valued the co-operation of local paediatricians and social workers.

'So I went to meet them,' she recalls. 'I've never felt such hostility. It was awful. I used to go to some of their meetings and they were very reticent about what they did. They wanted us to refer victims to them and we tried to tell them that we needed to know more about them – we agreed to differ on that.

'I was building up a relationship with them, but the chief constable was for some reason advised by one of his chief officers that really we shouldn't be doing this. So all the things we'd been trying to do for about three years just went. Oh, I wouldn't say it was a relationship that worked, but we'd reached an understanding. There was a personal problem. I tried to persuade them to be more feminine. I tried to tell them, "If you are good psychologists" – and they are excellent – "if you come to talk to our policemen in a nice blouse and skirt you'd win them over."'

She felt that her salvation arrived in the 1980s in the person of a young chief superintendent on his way up, Paul Whitehouse, who joined her at some of the meetings of local area review committees which planned policy and procedures for child abuse casework. 'He was the only one who ever did. The men often couldn't cope with area review committees because they thought they were airy-fairy. But they were important because they built up relationships and a process. So referrals to Tyneside Rape Crisis Centre then began to happen. He was able to change the procedures and there was a big shift in the attitudes in the police and in the TRCC, influencing each other's thinking. We all changed.'

Chief Superintendent Whitehouse ran the Northumbria force's community relations work in the early 1980s when the government instigated reviews of child abuse and sexual abuse procedures, and later became Chief Constable of Sussex Police. 'I felt it was important for me to go to the area review committees,' says Whitehouse, 'to indicate that it was an important function. One of the difficulties was about whether child sexual abuse should be written into the procedures.' There was resistance to that among police managers. 'Sexual abuse was seen as an area the public felt was so unpleasant that it had to be prosecuted, and if you were going to prosecute then you didn't need to worry about procedures, you just went ahead and prosecuted. We argued that this wasn't right and that we ought to have procedures. So they were written in gradually. Some difficulties came from other agencies. Sexual abuse is one of those things people don't like talking about, they don't believe it exists.

'What came over to me very strongly was that in the police service we had got it wrong in a very important fashion. We tended to say – and I don't think we were alone in this – that if a child reports abuse, take it out of the family. That was certainly the traditional way. Astonishing. I directed most of my attention to making sure that didn't happen.

'I was also wanting to get to know other agencies that were set up and campaigning, not so much against the police but for better treatment. I got involved with the Campaign for Homosexual Equality and I went to the TRCC. All the things they were saying I was agreeing with, because they were generally accurate. They were saying that women were not believed when they reported rape. And I said, "Correct." What they told us about the police was that we were uncaring – the usual things. They told me things I'd readily admit.' Despite prejudice against the TRCC – they were regarded as a bunch of lesbians – 'I carried on talking to them, because they existed. While they continued to make a noise it was my job to listen to them and take action where necessary. And more importantly, I wanted to persuade them that they had a duty to bring any woman who came along to us.'

Rhona Cross transmitted the TRCC's complaints through the police machinery. 'The TRCC were telling us their problems, perhaps about a policeman being rude to a woman, and we'd go to CID and tell them. Of course we were looked on as getting officers into trouble and that caused internal problems.'

The TRCC's roots in politics and in civil society rather than the professions and the state also meant that the police were dealing with a group 'who didn't play by the rules. Yet it worked,' said Rhona Cross. 'I always had great respect for their understanding and confidence, in the way they're trained and the way they think. But it is very difficult and unusual to construct a relationship with people who were completely unofficial. What I used to say was, "Look, we've got to talk to them because they're hearing about more cases of abuse than we are."'

In 1983 when the Home Office urged reform of the treatment of rape survivors, Cross and Whitehouse visited local hospitals to ask if the police could establish examination rooms there instead of in police stations. That same year, an idea emerged from the alliance between the police and the TRCC to recruit women doctors interested in sexual offences. About 35 women doctors joined what was to become the unique Women Police Doctors Group. Police surgeons didn't really approve. 'They said they'd been doing this for years, that they were trained. But their role wasn't really geared to this sort of crime,' said Rhona

Cross. 'And I don't think they really considered child sexual abuse. Of course, the women doctors were telling us all sorts of things about little girls' genitalia which I think the police surgeons really didn't know anything about. They don't really have a role in this. We were convinced that finance was the basis of a lot of this, because they'd lose money, you see. Money's got a lot to answer for.'

Today, Tyneside Rape Crisis Centre was housed in one of Newcastle-on-Tyne's handsome Victorian office blocks, with its own counselling suite and a serene reception room decorated like any modern woman's home. TRCC workers Elaine Snaith and Becket Ender tell their side of the story. 'When women came to us for counselling they'd tell us what they'd gone through if they'd gone to the police – which is always a minority of cases – and they told it as part of the trauma of being raped. It was very dramatic, the way women talked about it as being on a par with the first assault. They'd have to stand on a piece of brown paper to catch any debris and to maximise the amount of evidence, pubic hairs were plucked, there was an internal examination, and it all took place in the police station. The old male police surgeons were covering a multitude of sins, their training was forensic, it wasn't to sensitise them to the issue and to the woman.'

Rape crisis centres came out of the culture of the modern Women's Liberation Movement and often mirrored much of feminism's alienation from the structures of the state. The women remembered with wry smiles, that, 'The TRCC used to have a pseudonym, because when we started there was secrecy surrounding rape crisis centres' locations and around who was actually on the phone. The police were also making ridiculous demands in those days; they probably felt that some of our demands were ridiculous, too. But they wanted to know our names and addresses, to make sure they weren't recommending women to potential abusers. We had a secret address and a collective pseudonym for all of us, Beryl Thompson. God knows where the name came from – Beryl the Peril? The police or the media would ring and ask us for Beryl Thompson. Poor lass, she was always there, 24 hours a day, seven days a week. Anyway, we had a serious meeting with the police in a pub – neutral territory – and one of them asked if Beryl was present, and one woman said, "Er, yes . . ." while another said, "No, she's off sick . . ." So there was a lot of laughter and that was the atmosphere in which we came together. They knew Beryl didn't exist, but every time they called they asked for her and she – we – would be there. The thing was, we were breaking new ground and we had to be firmer than we would now because so many doors have been opened.

'Part of the reason we feel passionately about our policies is because of our experience as women: all of us are involved in trying to stop sexual abuse and to provide a service around that. In the police, there has been a gradual move towards service provision, with the police taking more responsibility for the role of the officers on site. Their line always used to be that they'd got to investigate a crime, they couldn't take the soft approach, couldn't spend resources on a story that would be thrown out of court in half an hour, couldn't take the hours it would take to pander to a woman who they thought was up a tree anyway, so what they needed was hard facts. And we'd say yes, but, but, but . . . They began to see that they could get more effective results. Crime figures were showing rapes unsolved. So they began to look at what was actually going on in the police stations.

'The framework was set for us by the Thames Valley documentary – we'd been involved in conversations with the police in the 1970s, but there probably wasn't a willingness on either side to let the barriers down, and there wasn't the skill to find a way in to each other. Where we started to find common ground was on child sexual abuse, whereas with rape we'd always seemed to be in opposition. It was an odd feeling.'

Child sexual abuse had already found its way into the TRCC's work – 60 per cent of the TRCC's clients were women who came to disinter the trauma not of recent rape but of abuse buried in childhood and often disclosed only by a fear that their own children might be, or were being, abused by their own father. This discovery quickly informed the centre's political objectives, not least because its internal discipline was based on assimilating women's lived experience and learning from it, rather than shrouding clients with preconceived expertise.

The TRCC regarded the Women Police Doctors Group as 'a major shift in ways of organising. The shift was inherited from the early Women's Liberation Movement philosophy of women organising together and providing their own resources. That had implications for people whose philosophy was for "experts". There's value in expertise, of course, but the resistance to it did have insights. About 30 women doctors were meeting and talking it all over and learning. The old methods of the men had meant that they didn't meet to discuss service provision around sexual assault. That was the major difference. And because of men's individualistic way of organising, they didn't cotton on. That's about fear, fear of losing control. That's where the police are still at, even though they've drafted in officers who are operationally flexible.'

Even now, there is a push in police forces to incorporate the work of rape crisis centres into their own structures, into police victim support schemes, rather than the police learning to live with the autonomy of groups whose sense of self is always rooted in a political culture of dissent.

The Women Police Doctors Group, too, developed its own way of organising, although it is well integrated with police networks. 'We treasured this thing we'd set up,' says Rhona Cross. Almost immediately, the group, which had been set up to service adult women, found itself deluged with children. 'We hadn't been seeing child sex abuse before. We knew it was going on, but we weren't addressing ourselves to it. When girls ran away we never thought they were running away because of interference by a male in the family. You didn't ask.'

Once the force did address itself to child sexual abuse, it set up six specialist child protection units headed by detective sergeants and staffed largely by women. Child abuse has moved from the province of community relations to CID, serious crime. This means that more and more women are being drawn into criminal investigations work, where once there were few.

Walking into Newcastle's West End Central unit is a little like where Hill Street Blues meets Cagney and Lacey, only with less noise and no guns. Half a dozen police officers have been trained in child abuse after coming from general police duties, ranging from burglary and traffic to sudden death. They explain that their priorities are 'protecting the child and sorting out who's done it. But the most important thing is protection of the child. You ensure that the child is going to be okay by working closely with social services, and making sure that the alleged perpetrator can't harm her any more. You either arrest him or take her to a place of safety. If you get a disclosure, it's fine, but you don't always get that. So we and the social workers interview the child together, maybe for weeks, because the child is reluctant to say who's done it. We've been working with one nine-year-old girl, for example, who told her mammy a bit about abuse in the past, but after medical evidence showed recent anal abuse she wouldn't say who'd done it. With all the programmes on television children are very wise, they know what is going to happen if anybody has assaulted them. They're not silly, these children, and there can be all sorts of reasons why they don't want to see the person go to prison.

'The job is about gaining the child's confidence and building a relationship. You can't ask leading questions, so we chat about everything and nothing. You have to reassure the child that everything will be all right, that she's the most important person and you've got to convince her that she's done nothing wrong, that you are her friend and you believe her. They're not daft, they know when you are not interested and don't really want to work with them. You have to give a lot of time to it, as much time as we can spare. It's totally different to anything we've ever done, it's not like burglary or a sudden death, it's not going to last an hour or two – you could spend six weeks working with a child.

'But it can be very frustrating. A file may go to the Crown Prosecution Service, who decide whether or not to prosecute, with 'Insufficient Evidence' written on it, and that's that. In our job, unless you get a confession or unless you get really fantastic evidence and the child is over eleven years old and, therefore can give evidence on oath, then there's nothing. It's frustration, frustration. Sometimes we're very annoyed in here because the file gets closed: "no further action". We moan, we groan – and we get pissed on Friday night.

'So we've got a system in this unit, we get over all our frustrations, we get our bad moods out of the window before we go out of the door to our own homes. We talk about it all and we look after each other.'

What the Northumbria police had to learn, however, was that child protection had to be their priority. 'We felt we must go in there and support social services in what they were doing to protect the child. Protection came before prosecution as a priority.'

That was the lesson Cleveland constabulary had not learned before 1987.

Leeds – child sex rings

It was fortuitous that Inspector Trevor Buckroyd had finished his Open University humanities course when he was posted to a new police station in south Leeds, in the West Yorkshire police force, in the early 1980s. He was already in the last lap of his police career, so he wasn't looking for promotion either – child sexual abuse wasn't promotional material. When he arrived at his new position, he consulted his sergeant, David Giles, about policing priorities: Giles suggested that child abuse would benefit from more police time and attention.

Sooner rather than later they found themselves with a case for which they had not been prepared either by their new-found interest or their police training. The case unearthed 17 sex rings involving 21 men, who were ultimately prosecuted, and more than 200 children aged from eight to sixteen. It was one of the biggest rings ever discovered in Britain and consumed the working, waking and sometimes the sleeping lives of the police team – Buckroyd, Giles and two WPCs, Martina Fletcher and Karina Quayle – for two years, as they toiled largely alone with colleagues in social services, education and paediatrics. And it led to the creation of three specialist child protection units. Trevor Buckroyd reckons that child sexual abuse 'isn't there if you don't look for it. But once you set up a unit, you get the calls.'

The team had to learn not only new techniques of detection, but also new modes of co-operation with and dependence on other professionals. Politically, they also had to make what society would regard as risky decisions about policing and protection priorities: did their obligations lie with their own profession, with the child, or with the family?

The first sex ring was uncovered both by the police and social services in April 1984 when a girl had a skirmish with a five-year-old boy while she was babysitting. His mother came home to find him terribly upset, bruised and with a lacerated penis. When Giles and Buckroyd saw the girl, she 'admitted the bruising but not the penis. Our eyes met across the table and we knew it was sexual abuse of some sort.' It turned out that the girl was infuriated by the boy playing with his penis: she was fed up with willies! During her interview she disclosed that she was a regular visitor to a man for whom, in return for small rewards – a few pennies or cigarettes – she traded her body. And if they didn't believe her, they could ask her friend, who was also a regular visitor.

Within weeks other rings were uncovered. 'In the beginning,' says Trevor Buckroyd, 'we didn't in all honesty know what we'd unearthed. Names came to us day by day. We didn't understand the scale of it, neither did social services. It got called child prostitution. We didn't like that. We didn't know what it was, but we didn't like that. So by the time we got to intra-familial abuse in Leeds, we'd already cut our teeth on the sex rings. I went through the barrier of disbelief.'

Unlike most cases of child sexual abuse, sex rings provide unique threads of corroboration. One child leads to another. Children were recruited by other children, and the children's own networks provided the investigators with crucial corroboration. But this didn't cure the south Leeds investigators of their inhibitions. 'As a police officer I found it very difficult to accept that what I was hearing had in fact taken place, because they were talking about sexual relations which, quite frankly, I didn't think could or would happen. Most significant for me was they were doing it not purely for (but not regardless of) attention – there was a genuine seeking for personal worth,' says Buckroyd. But if a sense of worthlessness might have been the cause, it was also the effect.

How had these children been perceived before? Certainly they, and generations before them, had been coralled into a culture of abuse which was both known and accepted. Curiously, child sexual abuse, or molestation, has been reserved in our society in a special category of crime – one of the ultimate outrages which has been mobilised perennially in defence of ultimate punishments. But what the Leeds sex rings revealed was that child sexual abuse was also integrated into a community's sense of itself. It wasn't as if there hadn't been clues – clues enough if anyone had been curious: 'We checked back through old records and found that five or six girls had gone missing from home on 20 or 30 occasions.' And on Friday nights – when the abuser paid more for a girl to stay the night. The only difference between then and now was that the police had decided to do something.

That in itself was a cultural revolution. 'There's a long-held belief in the police service,' says Buckroyd, 'that you act on a complaint, you don't act to get a complaint. The corporate approach in the police service was and is – and it's brought about by police training – if she's not telling you, then there's no complaint, and if she's not complaining, why bother? What's the hassle?'

Those homilies didn't help the team. How were they to

intervene? The difficulties were sometimes compounded by the police surgeons, who, unlike the city's paediatricians, were solely concerned with seeking signs on the body. 'They don't give time for anything other than physical signs. We were happier with the paediatricians in Leeds who looked at the child as a whole, rather than at a particular part of the anatomy', says Buckroyd.

'Then there's the secrecy, the element of complicity, which makes it even more difficult. If I'm honest, it wasn't until we started bringing in prisoners and started talking about gross indecency and other serious charges that our credibility was upheld. If you've been hours interviewing kids and you haven't come up with a body or a complaint, where's your credibility? I remember I went to a retirement do where there were the CID lads. I remember being pulled up at the bar by a retired officer, very senior, and told that up there in south Leeds it had been going on for years: "They'll always take a florin from somebody to put their hand down her knickers." When you've got your back to the wall, who's going to believe the word of an eight-year-old about an adult man? And all over the city people were saying, "It's south Leeds! It's Slagsville!"'

Trevor Buckroyd also had to confront his own prejudices about women during this work with children. As a result, he came to defend the practice, which is disavowed elsewhere, of officers interviewing both the abused and the abusers. His reasons seem to have as much to do with respect for the initial investigators – often women who tend to operate in community development rather than CID – as for the investigation itself. Child sexual abuse often originates with community liaison staff and is then transferred to CID, causing considerable confusion for the public, who feel they never know who is actually handling a case, as well as for the investigators who do the donkey work only to be deprived of the consummation. Community liaison is regarded as soft – a place for women and people with A-levels. CID is for real men and real crime. This division has often robbed men of the subtleties of serving their communities, and has likewise tended to leave women quarantined outside the pale of prestigious criminal work. Trevor Buckroyd recalls, 'I remember coming in one day and saying to Dave Giles, "Where are the girls?" meaning the other policewomen. He said they'd gone to pull in So-and-so. I froze. We'd sent two women out! They weren't the Sunday Palladium picture of policewomen, they were young, quite attractive. That was my traditionalist attitude. Dave said, "Why not? Why shouldn't they have the satisfaction of finishing the job?" And I agreed.'

It was the network of corroboration which overcame the disbelief. But if that didn't overcome the obstacles to gathering evidence, it did modify detection. Initially, a police officer might feel animated by anger: 'You have the knowledge of the horrible things done to the child and you want to do something about it.' But that would often get in the way of long, labour-intensive inquiries which banished anger, put a premium on patience and put an impossible price on police time.

'In the past you'd give the girl a couple of hours. If that failed to come up with something, you'd have a word with the guy. But what you've done is heighten the risk factor. Because by then he's convinced the police he's not involved. He's wary. Extra wary. You don't get many shots at disclosure and if you cock that up you cause additional despair, or you opt out before they're ready to talk. Bluntly, you can't do this work successfully without an element of risk, and the risk takes bottle, because you're saying you've not got enough information yet, and you've got to learn to live with robbing a child of its liberty in order to make it safe, and that can't be done until the child is separated from the abuser.

'Our training tells us that we should not interview children, even as witnesses, without their parents being present. But you can't expect a girl to be forthcoming in front of her parents if the abuse is intra-family – how can she say what's happened, knowing it will shatter the family? I can't think of anything more difficult. That's why you get a high rate of retractions. Retraction is part of the overall thing. When the child realises the enormity of it, she often retracts.

'With many of the children we had to work very hard to show rapport, to show that we knew they'd been drawn into something they didn't want to do. Sometimes they were *adamant* that nothing had happened, when we knew it had. The kids, they're not happy to tell you what they've been involved in. And the moment you show revulsion or horror you've lost her, because she knows in her mind that it's bloody awful and that maybe she had a choice and took the wrong choice. She'll test you to see if you'll *judge her*. Even if you say "Dirty bugger" then it'll start running away from her, and ultimately from you. If there is any sense of complicity or guilt, and there often is, then you are always being tested.

'The family is behind four walls so the relationship is an enclosed world and it follows that the majority of known abused children will come from lower-class families, because for many other reasons they are monitored. One of the reasons we were successful was because we were looking at families who were causing concern to other agencies perhaps for other reasons, like truancy, tantrums. The family is a protected ethic and this is what the MP Stuart Bell is on about. The normal residence is out of public view. The classic situation – the attack on the child in a public park – will cause shock and horror, but the same attack *inside* the home is another world. Certainly one of the regular comments made to us, for all the good we were doing, was, "Well, what do you expect in south Leeds?" Look at the more middle-class areas, they're more adept at covering up, they hide their skeletons better. We saw ourselves as speaking for a child who'd not had an opportunity to be heard as an individual.'

As detectives, the Leeds team had to learn a new kind of listening. 'What the person in the street would expect is that you gave the abuser a hard time, shouting and threatening – and *he'd* expect that, too. But the opposite would apply, because nobody wants to sit down and tell you readily what they've done with young children. The likelihood is that in a one-to-one situation the child gives you the circumstances when they're akin to an attack. She'll not readily describe a seduction process, a bribery process. But if that's how she wants to tell it, that's how we'll record it. We kept them talking. We recorded every single detail, both in their manner and in their content. By giving time to the kids – you see they don't know what you want to know – you can learn the lifestyle of the abuser. Perhaps you're not in there with a chance of prosecution, but if you've got a lot of apparently incidental information you can unravel it before him. All but three of the 21 abusers pleaded guilty. The main thing is to keep them talking. I don't have any particular feelings about the men. By trying to do the best possible professional job for the child, I think we managed to avoid any extreme feelings one way or another about the men.

'Cleveland made me go cold. It smacked of everything we'd tried not to do,' said Buckroyd. 'We work closely with social services and educational welfare – the key to it all is *planned intervention* because it is so reassuring to everybody involved. We all need each other so much. It's an issue that has thrown up so much professional arrogance, not least in our own force. We have to say as a police service we've not done this work very well in the past. All complaints went to CID, so you were asking an overworked department to take on something requiring a heavy time input. Officers just haven't the time, or perhaps the will, or the ability. It's such a unique area of work.'

Not surprisingly, many police forces stumbled into it, bringing only their own traditions. According to Det. Insp. Keith Lawrence who supervised child sexual abuse work in West Yorkshire, which incorporates Leeds, 'There were the dinosaurs who always wanted results. They'd compare child sexual abuse with a burglary, and only recently it is being accepted that it takes a different kind of person to do detection work in this field.'

The sex rings taught the Buckroyd team that 'We've got to always bear in mind our responsibility to the safety of that child. It's not just about pursuing the case through to a prosecution. Many's the time when we just hung on in there in support of social services, to assist in care proceedings, in the knowledge that it would never get to criminal court.' That meant staying involved but subordinating the police imperatives to those of the other professionals, 'and that was difficult to communicate to some bobbies – and bosses! – that we were co-operating in order to support other agencies.

'A declared intent of ours was to stick with social services, even though it wasn't necessarily going to lead to a prosecution. The problem of child sex abuse demands a re-think by all the agencies about their work and about reconciling their working practices. And we have to look at the motives for not sharing information. Do the police recognise the significance of and the real reasons why children go missing from home? Is the police job just limited to returning a girl to the bosom of her family? Is the social worker involved with a family concerned that the information will lead to the break-up of the family, which they don't want because it suggests failure on their part? Is the teacher, having met the parents in the best setting, accepting the child's hints as fiction not fact?'

For around two years the core of officers involved worked long hours, sometimes 16 hours a day, without any sources of support other than each other. 'I didn't want or need the overtime, but the way I felt some mornings when I crept out of bed! No money was going to compensate for how rough we felt. We had an unofficial agreement among ourselves: even if it was one o'clock in the morning before we finished work, we'd never just walk out of the station and drive to our homes. We never consumed alcohol, so we'd sit in that office with a coffee and almost without exception there'd be various incidents in the day that were hilarious. That became part of our day-to-day routine. We had a team and we shared this end-of-the-day ritual together. I don't know what the social workers did, but we certainly found a need to encompass the ones who had an empathy with us in our little tryst.'

Notes

1 Metropolitan Police and Bexley Social Services, *Child Sexual Abuse, Joint Investigative Programme, The Bexley Experiment*, Final Report, London: HMSO, 1987.

2 I was helped to think through the politics of evidence by Helen Birch and her unpublished MA thesis on women and murder mysteries, *The Women Who Knew Too Much*, University of Sussex, 1984.

3 Metropolitan Police and Bexley Social Services, *ibid.*

4 Roland Barthes, 'The Photographic Message' in *Image-Media-Text*, London, 1977.

5 Rosalind Coward, *Female Desire*, London, 1984.

6 John Berger, *Ways of Seeing*, London, 1972.

7 Metropolitan Police and Bexley Social Services, *ibid.*

8 Sandra Jones, *Policewomen and Equality*, London, 1986.

9 Cleveland Refuge and Aid for Women and Children, 1984.

10 London Rape Crisis Centre, *Sexual Violence*, London: 1984, quoting Police Review 1975.

POLITICS – PUBLIC AND PRIVATE

'State Power' and 'Parent Power'

'It was a situation of fairly uncontrolled panic. Fear was rife up and down the corridors. Everything other than child abuse was put on "pending". By the last week of June when the media attention was intense, social services began to get their act together. But in terms of *what* we were doing it was panic. Getting a social worker to see a child who wasn't abused was enormously difficult,' recalled one social worker posted at Cleveland's social services headquarters in Marton House near Middlesbrough town centre during the crisis. That crisis had changed so much in the relationship between 'the people' and professionals – for it generated an unprecedented, organised challenge to the authority and autonomy of professions supposed to be servicing the people.

'We were aware of the crisis by what social workers were telling us, about the lawyers acting as spokespeople for the parents. We were aware that we had no resources but we couldn't afford to be losing cases at that point. A lot of social workers had to become very expert very quickly. Each day at Marton House there were what were called war cabinet meetings of senior management to review case developments, police action (or usually the absence of it), possible problems in the courts, areas where we needed social workers to give solid evidence. War cabinet memos were being issued daily to area officers and team leaders on how to manage the crisis.'

The number of the doctors' diagnoses had increased from a handful in the first few months of the year to scores in May and June. The anxious social worker felt that, 'All Cleveland had done was appoint an adviser. She was given no resources to set up an infrastructure until the crisis. The phrase one social worker uttered to me in a moment of desperation was, "We're making it up as we go along." Senior managers were putting in seven days a week, 12 hours a day, meeting in each other's houses after they'd got away. Managers were saying to each other, "Where do we stand on this one?" and one plaintive cry from someone expected to act professionally without the framework to do it was, "Where's the system?"

'People were cringing every night before the television. Issues were fought out there and in the papers. I thought to myself, I'm reading this, feeling like this, but what about 12- or 13-year-olds watching television – is all this going to make them want to disclose? But for all that, on the evidence put before me – and I looked at a lot of cases – there wasn't a single case that I felt wasn't valid and that we shouldn't fight.'

That feeling reverberated among most of the social services department's staff who, despite the overwhelming national criticism, never broke ranks. But it reveals the *politics* at stake in *procedures*, and the conflicting interests at work in the local state.

The rocky road to crisis in 1987 began several years earlier. Since the early 1980s there had been no consensus between Cleveland social services, police and the probation service on prosecution policy in the county. Like every other region, it had an Area Review Committee to co-ordinate policy among the relevant agencies, and it began to modernise procedures for child abuse. However, negotiations on joint investigations by police and other child protection staff, and joint examinations between police surgeons and other doctors, including paediatricians, stalled year after year when police managers threw out provisional agreements on co-operation. According to evidence given to the inquiry by social worker Rita Summerbell, police officers seemed to turn up at each meeting only to repudiate what social workers thought had been agreed at the last one.

The county's caring agencies, however, had not been unaware of sexual abuse, nor of the need to make procedures match new awareness of its prevalence or the enduring pain it caused its victims. South Tees Area Health Authority, for example, had for several years employed two health visitors, Marjorie Dunn and Freda Roach, as senior nurses and designated officers for child abuse. They met depressing indifference from some of their colleagues in other professions. Apart from taking part in a growing number of case conferences, they had also helped set up an informal core group of professionals in the county to alert the community to sexual abuse, often through talking to mothers, as well as colleagues, and to encourage training among nurses, teachers, social workers, doctors and the police.

In July 1985 they invited education and social services, police officers, nurses, doctors, the school medical service, psychologists and psychiatrists to the first meeting of the Child Sexual Abuse Training Co-ordination Group. They were disappointed by the response – only a handful of representatives from social services, the National Society for the Prevention of Cruelty to Children (NSPCC) and

117

education turned up. Notable for their absence were psychiatrists, the police and doctors. Undaunted, they prepared proposals for the county's designated officers the following September, but again met indifference. The core group pressed ahead, organising educational work in schools, seminars for head teachers, and a special interest group among nurses.

Meanwhile, they had to take responsibility for real live cases. Marjorie Dunn recalled one of her first, involving a very young child taken into care, who began telling her foster parents about sexual abuse. 'How were we to deal with it, given a total denial by the named adult? We were stuck. We had to really fight to get them to take it through the courts – you see, in those days you didn't feel so helpless if you could get a prosecution. But sexual abuse is a very serious allegation to make against adults.

'We began to take strong decisions without all the procedures. The police officers in community relations in my Langbaugh district were very good, and they'd say to a child, "We believe you, we can't prosecute, but we believe you", and they'd co-operate in protecting the child. But that has all fallen apart because of the crisis.'

When the crisis began, Dunn and Roach were again to find themselves ignored by some of the major protagonists. Both women complained that, although responsible for monitoring the work in their districts, they weren't being told about children going into hospital and so couldn't help parents who approached them for information about their children. Case conferences, the crucial context for planning the care of children, kept being delayed because the consultants failed to provide diagnostic evidence and the police failed to co-operate.

Marjorie Dunn was to be described, or rather denigrated, at the end of the judicial inquiry as a 'forceful lady'. The term connected her with other women who became the subject of a whispering campaign which conjured them as the creators of the crisis. 'I've never in my life before been called forceful,' she said later, 'but I didn't like the inference.'

In the mid-1980s, the work of Marjorie Dunn and Freda Roach was beginning to be taken up by lone voices from the political left. In 1986 the somnolent Social Services Committee was nudged into action on child abuse by John Bell, the county's first elected councillor from a new generation of radicals who were beginning to transform the area's Labour Party.

John Bell was 25 when he was elected as a county councillor in the mid-1980s. He was from a background of respectable, working-class men 'who were unbelievably bad to their women', and he became part of the punk generation. 'It was the late 1970s and the Labour Party was up the Swanee. We had to take our lives in our own hands and do something,' he said, so while working as an electrician, he played in a band and got involved in politics. After his election he joined the county's Social Services Committee and made a priority of child abuse, 'because I'd known from school that lasses were sexually abused and lads were beaten up by their dads. I was a person who was in a responsible position, so I could do something about it.' Wandering around the social services department he discovered a library and began reading up on the issue. 'I must admit sometimes I couldn't carry on, I'd have to put the book down and pick it up later because I was absolutely appalled, I hadn't really known what it was all about.' John Bell's self-education and his efforts with another left-wing councillor who was also a electrician, Bob Pitt, to radicalise the county council was later to arouse the suspicion of Stuart Bell, MP. He claimed that social services were elitist empire-builders, and in his evidence to the inquiry alleged that social services were 'abetted in their search for new money by Councillors Bell and Pitt, both electricians by trade, each acquiring such a surprising knowledge of child abuse' that they were able to cite the classic texts on it. 'So,' commented John Bell, 'he was being elitist. He was clearly saying that because we're electricians we can't read things and we're thick.'

Cllr Bell found endorsement in the publication of Louis Blom-Cooper's stern rebuke of Brent social services after his investigation of the death of Jasmine Beckford. Social workers all over the country feared the effects of their own failure after he had accused individual social workers of not protecting Jasmine from mutilation and ultimately murder by her father. The Beckford report exposed both the professional and political problems of child protection following the shift into generic social work, which made social-work teams the Jacks and Jills of all trades.

By 1986, the new awareness of all forms of child abuse – battering, emotional terror and sexual exploitation – had outstripped resources, inter-agency arrangements and individual skills. Cleveland was cruelly to expose the lack of all three. Procedures had been universally acknowledged to be in need of urgent modernisation, because local authority structures had changed, and because the shift into generic social work had exposed the lack of specialisation and expertise in childcare. Child abuse demanded both general re-training, and a renaissance of specialisation in the very era in which social services were being starved of resources.

The Beckford report also threw down a political gauntlet – Jasmine's death had been 'predictable and avoidable', said Blom-Cooper, who insisted that local authorities must take responsibility as 'a trustee parent on behalf of the community which demands that the child be protected'. Ultimately it was our elected representatives who, though not directly involved in case management, were to take 'the prime and ultimate responsibility' for the fate of children. What Cleveland revealed was political inertia – the absence of child protection in the political agenda. Did society really demand that children be protected? And if so, from whom? And how?

Child torture came to haunt Thatcherism during the 1980s. The ghosts of dead children – Jasmine Beckford, Tyra Henry and Kimberley Carlile all destroyed by their fathers – smiled out from the newspapers, their photographs snipped from supposedly Happy Family albums, while the texts alongside described bites, burns, broken bones and then death. These little martyrs to bad, mad men were handed over to a populist politics of punishment. It all seemed to vindicate Thatcherism's scorn for the busy-body welfare state. But not quite: these children died within the family, the institution sanctified by Thatcherism. The state had sinned by omission, not commission – families were kept intact, and children were killed. Neither Blom-Cooper's report, nor the subtler investigation and critique of Lambeth social services' failure to protect Tyra Henry chaired by Stephen Sedley, QC, supported Thatcherism's anti-statism. They demanded that social services be positive, rather than passive, in the protection of children at risk.[1]

Cleveland's strategy

That was exactly what Cleveland County embarked on towards the end of 1986 when in October Sue Richardson took up her post as one of the first post-Beckford child abuse consultants in the country. But she was working with antique arrangements. For more than a decade there had been a national consensus in favour of streamlining childcare law but no new national guidelines had been issued. Local authorities, whether in calm or crisis, were making it up as they went along.

Sue Richardson was a child of the welfare state and the 1944 Education Act. She was a clever girl, the daughter of 'unskilled' working-class parents, both of whom had gone to grammar schools before the Second World War but whose families couldn't afford to keep them in school. Her mother particularly emphasised education as her children's route out of her own disappointments. For many mothers of Sue Richardson's generation, there was usually something that symbolised mothers' ruin – in her case it was cleaning windows that signified waste of a woman's life. Sue Richardson embarked on a social work career that was consonant with the moral and political mores of her family. Methodism and Labourism defined its sense of social responsibility, much as it had defined a strong seam of British socialism. Methodism meant you took personal responsibility for your world and Labourism defined class loyalty – you never betrayed the working class.

Sexual abuse came into her career because, 'If you work with families then you will find a lot of child abuse. I didn't seek it out, the work found me. My odyssey was to integrate frameworks and beliefs, and my search is for what produces change in people. I was always looking for something that was effective in producing change.' Her experience of social work and family therapy led her to adopt a tough approach to sexual abuse strategies which moved away from the 'let's-all-have-a-nice-voluntary-agreement' sort of approach. 'With dangerous families you can't do that. You actually have to take power, and I believe that's right. Paradoxically, I found, and they've found this elsewhere, that by taking a more authoritative – some would say a more authoritarian – stance at the beginning, families can gain greater freedom in the end. Because if you can hold them in therapeutic work for long enough to do the work they need to do, they can gain their autonomy, get out from under.'

She had already experienced managerial angst before taking up her consultant's post. 'Our managers were frightened, because we started making demands, you see, we demanded good management, and resources, and a mandate for our work which was about producing change.'

It was the complex pressure of trying to create new structures, working with real live families and coping with management fears which prompted her to move into management herself and to design frameworks for action. 'The problem with local authorities is that they're not geared to risk-taking adventurous work or creativity, so it's very hard to survive within them. They're not therapeutic organisations, they're not about producing change, they're about maintaining the status quo.'

She defended what appeared to be a heavy approach to children's safety. 'I've always taken a very positive view, even in the most horrendous situations – I work on people's strengths rather than their weaknesses. I would look at what had caused a situation, but I wouldn't think it was always going to be like that in any and every situation. You see, I'm interested in what enables people to change, to recover and overcome their difficulties. I hate the way a lot of professionals have very set ways of labelling parents, so they're never able to get rid of the label, to heal and rehabilitate themselves.

'I do have firm ideas about the context of our work, and I think that's why people get very confused about me.

I might take a stance that is firmly non-negotiable in the beginning, because I believe that with dangerous families you do need power, and you might look pretty draconian at first. But I don't have set ideas about people and about what they can and can't achieve. And apparently people can't appreciate those subtleties. I want clarity about the framework. I don't like things being left in the shadow of suspicion. I hate the kind of social work that is about monitoring and policing people.

'What has been eclipsed in this whole thing is that we were overwhelmed with numbers. We started with a philosophy of using power, because you're dealing with what Susanne Sgroi calls a "disorder of power", and therefore you have to have enough power to deal with it. What we had tended to do was take enough power to try to sort the situation out. It was never intended to leave it at that, but unfortunately during the crisis we weren't able to do the work we wanted to do. The whole idea had been to give the children breathing space – remember, we were dealing with a situation in which the children weren't ready to disclose. We'd hoped to use place of safety orders to keep the children with caring, neutral adults, and then get them back home. And we didn't know who in the child's household – if anyone at all – we were supposed to be protecting them from. We didn't have the resources, we weren't able to do enough work and also perhaps we weren't sufficiently skilled.

'Police hostility was absolutely crucial. People say the multi-disciplinary system broke down – it did, but only in the sense that the police weren't prepared to be part of it. The work was quite highly developed here, but the police weren't part of it. That's probably true all over the country – the police don't have very flexible boundaries, and they tend not to cross their own boundaries. You go to them, they don't go to you. They're almost a law unto themselves, very self-contained, very autonomous. That worries me, because they're not as accountable as other agencies.'

That still worried social services and doctors a year after the crisis erupted, when despite the creation of a special unit to deal with sexual abuse, the police still seemed to be going it alone.

It wasn't only a hostile media which reacted against Cleveland social services strategy. Criticism came, too, from feminists for whom sexual abuse was part of a bigger sexual politics, and who felt that it was wrong to remove the child rather than the abuser from the home. Sue Richardson felt, however, that action had to be taken to protect children where the social services department had no mandate to remove an alleged abuser, even if a person had been named. Where they could, the department tried to work out 'protection packages', usually with the women in families, and usually involving a father's voluntary absence from the home, although these were not always sanctioned by the hospital.

On her arrival in Cleveland, Sue Richardson swiftly set about creating the networks for a new era. There was no therapeutic resource easily accessible for sexually abused children. There was no short-stay space for children needing sanctuary, and the number of hospital beds for children, which might provide temporary respite, had been cut by two-thirds. A police working party appeared not to be meeting, and so a sub-committee was set up by Sue Richardson to resume the review of procedures. At the same time, she complained to the police about their dilatory presence at case conferences, which were crucial to joint strategic planning by all the caring agencies involved.

There were still no updated guidelines for the investigation of allegations of abuse. But by 1986, child abuse was deemed the department's 'most serious issue'. The county's arrangements were described by a working party as 'superficially good' but suffering from some instances of 'weakness and confusion'. Cleveland was known to rely heavily on 'place of safety orders' (PSOs) which gave the council the power to place children in protected environments – with other relatives, in foster homes, children's homes or hospitals – for up to 28 days. Congestion in the courts often made the proceedings a marathon. According to a county legal officer responsible for children, 'Delay was built into the system.' Nevertheless Cleveland had always favoured the stringencies of PSOs because, he says, 'using the courts is a way of ensuring things don't drift. There's a deeply held belief among my colleagues that we should be seen to be publicly accountable, that we should give parents and ourselves a public forum – the courts – in which to consider the child's future. It is not a strategy to get children into care, because we're not paid by the number of kids in care, but for taking positive decisions at an early stage – care proceedings focus on the needs of the child.'

In February 1987 the county council's Social Services Committee agreed that child abuse was its 'number one priority' and agreed to allocate an extra £80,000 to develop specialists – half the sum the professionals had been bidding for. No sooner had the committee processed this project than the county council's commitment was tested. But not, contrary to myth, by the arrival of Dr Marietta Higgs at Middlesbrough General the previous month, nor by her alleged conspiracy with Sue Richardson to exclude the police surgeon. Sue Richardson's commitment to joint investigation was exemplified in the first critical case to present itself in February, when Dr Joyce Longwill examined a child during one of her school clinics and found physical signs arousing suspicions of sexual abuse. She contacted Sue Richardson to share her worries and seek advice, and Dr Higgs and Dr Irvine were called in to conduct a joint examination together. This seemed to satisfy everyone. But it was the conduct of the police inquiries which fouled up this collaboration. They arrested the child's grandfather, only to find that a month later Dr Higgs suspected she had been abused again. The child named her father. He was never interviewed by the police. Dr Irvine told a case conference that he believed anal dilatation could be found in 'normal' children and on the strength of that the police told a 22 March case conference that there was insufficient evidence to prosecute and they'd be pulling out. This was the first case of what was to become the crisis, and the first multi-disciplinary collapse.

By May the county council was unable in some cases to enforce PSOs. One family of children, for example, had been taken to hospital by their mother. Their head teacher had called in social services after noticing blood in one of the children's knickers. Sexual abuse was suspected. The father, who had been given no access by the court, joined the melee in Ward 9 and removed them for several days. After he had been reassured by a police surgeon that there were believed to be no signs of abuse, the father returned the children to the hospital, where they were again diagnosed as showing signs of abuse. A spiral of second and more opinions ensued. In the end they went home.

The police had, in practice, pulled out – despite, in one case, being urged to carry on by the parents themselves. Sue Richardson proposed that the working party she had set up to review procedures be called together to resolve the differences. But others felt that given past problems in negotiations with the police, there was no point. Although co-operation between individual police and social services officers continued in some areas, relationships appeared to have broken down at management level by the beginning of May, many weeks before both sides formally decided to go it alone. It was that managerial breach which began to poison relationships among rank-and-file workers.

By May, Sue Richardson knew that the number of referrals was likely to multiply rapidly, and she warned her manager, Bill Walton, the number two in the social services department, of the resource difficulties this was going to create for the department. Walton, however, decided that the department could probably cope – a fatally flawed prognosis. By the end of the month the department was running out of safe places to put the children and was desperately canvassing other agencies for facilities. Without much luck. Aware of the rumbles of controversy, they wanted to wait and see.

At this stage, the conflict over the diagnosis, until now a diplomatic incident, erupted into war. On 28 May representatives of social services, the police and the paediatricians met, apparently to finalise new multi-disciplinary guidelines. The childcare professionals present felt impatient with what was, by now, a long history of attrition, with both the police and the police surgeon refusing to relinquish control over the investigation of child sexual abuse – a concession other police forces had already made, in recognition of the limited options for prosecution.

In Cleveland, of course, it was a contest over both control and the very concept of widespread abuse. On 29 May Sue Richardson prepared a memorandum which was issued in the name of her director, Mike Bishop, which made it clear that the county would continue to take protective action if children were referred by the paediatricians, and that the county would go ahead without a second opinion from a police surgeon. In other contexts, such a procedure might not have seemed so provocative – other social service departments and police authorities had relied on paediatricians, and Northumberland police worked with their own squad of specialist women doctors and a group of paediatricians based in Gateshead. But in Cleveland the furore over the diagnosis polluted professional relationships. Richardson's memorandum was, in the end, read as a red rag to a bull. Mike Bishop remained loyal to Sue Richardson throughout the controversy, which was more than many a manager might have done in the circumstances. He later defended the memorandum as the only option available.

Mike Bishop had more than decency on his side. At the beginning of the year, the government had issued a White Paper, *The Law on Child Care and Family Service*, which suggested streamlining the much-criticised legal devices available to local authorities, and replacing the Place of Safety Orders by an Emergency Protection Order. This would be for only eight days, as opposed to the 28 days allowed by PSOs. (The majority of Cleveland's PSOs were for 28 days, which was criticised by some commentators as draconian.) The White Paper also insisted that the objective was to protect children: it supported local authorities taking children into care in the face of the 'absence or incapacity of parents', and urged on them a 'more active duty to investigate'.

Although the White Paper, typically, failed to face up to the potential conflict of interest between promoting child protection and preventing the breakdown of family relationships, it reiterated the duty of local authorities to investigate and intervene on *suspicion* of child abuse. That was all the local authority had ever done. 'The protection of children was unmanageable unless we took action,' Mike Bishop told the inquiry. 'Otherwise the children would simply be returned home, and I was not prepared to countenance that until I was satisfied that it was safe for them.'

Asked during the inquiry whether he should not have sailed between the extremes in the diagnostic debate, Bishop stoically defended his department's refusal to back away from the diagnosis. 'Given that at the height of the crisis we did not have the resources to do the investigations that we do now, and which I regard as good practice, and which I think is common ground between us, how on earth could I decide, "This diagnosis is right and that one may be wrong"? How do you expect me, as a director of social services, to do that? If I did it, if I tried to do it and I got it wrong, what would you be saying to me now?'

As it happened, a clear – and perhaps surprising – endorsement of the diagnosis emerged during the inquiry, contrary to the clear impression given by the media. While courts throughout the country became sceptical of anal dilatation as grounds for suspecting sexual abuse, Mrs Justice Butler-Sloss and her panel of advisers knew that they would be vindicating it. It might have embarrassed them to know that one day they were going to have to say so, given the state of public opinion. But embarrassment began to ebb away from Marton House – the department had fulfilled the duty to act on suspicion, even if the diagnosis was 'suspect'. It believed it was doing what the White Paper mandated it to do – intervene.

28 May was to become emblematic of the crisis throughout the inquiry: it was preoccupied with blame for the fracas and its consequences. Dr Irvine shouted that Dr

Higgs was incompetent, rubbished the diagnosis and stormed out threatening that they could expect to receive writs. On 29 May social services drafted a memorandum reiterating its commitment to act on the paediatricians' diagnosis of suspected abuse by seeking place of safety orders. But why were children removed? Why does the detection of sexual crime always seem to demand the evacuation of the victims rather than the culprits? Why were so many children removed in Cleveland, rather than suspected abusers?

Bill Walton crystallised the county council's dilemma when he told the inquiry that the memo would not have been issued if there had not been the row on 28 May. With the department's resources already overstretched, 'we did not have the staff to do the job that I would normally expect and want to be done, which is investigation – and I would put emphasis on investigation – before we take any action.' Asked whether, in the absence of investigation, 'the only solution is inflexible intervention?', Bill Walton replied, 'No. It is to protect.' Although he was never a fan of 28-day orders, he said, he could not countenance 'what may be the return of that child to an abusing situation. Until I am firmly convinced of who has undertaken the abuse it is very difficult. So some protective action is required until full investigation can be carried out. That is the object of the place of safety order – to allow time to investigate.'

The department did not, however, simply put its trust in the diagnosis. It called in Dr Higgs on 1 June and gave her the third degree. She was 'very cool and convincing,' said Mike Bishop. The department also tried to persuade her to slow down the rate of referral – she refused. And early in June Mike Bishop met with the chief constable to repair the row with the police. He failed. Sue Richardson

131

reckoned that most of her time was subsequently spent 'mobilising resources'.

Social workers at work

Cleveland's Family Centre, a relatively autonomous facility staffed by a group of local authority social workers, was one of those to experience truculence from the police where before there had been comfortable camaraderie. But the police weren't their only problem. They felt that Dr Higgs didn't heed their strategic suggestions either. The absence of a culture of intra-professional consultation left these social workers feeling that even though they might be sympathetic to Dr Higgs' project, their own wisdoms were not being respected.

'We feel betrayed by other professionals,' said one of them. 'Dr Higgs is good, and we feel she's done good work for us, but the grief it has all caused has been so profound and so enormous. And the police haven't co-operated. At first we didn't know it was a crisis. We have had several cases of sexual abuse, where we were sure the children had been abused. For a year a lot of us here had been going on courses, so we had it on our minds. We had one family which seemed to be functioning adequately for a while and then a number of things gave us cause for concern around May. We thought it was all falling apart. A GP rang us and said a woman had brought a baby to see him, she feared the father might be interfering with the little girl and he said the child should be examined. We said we wouldn't be surprised if abuse was happening because just about everything else was and the mother had complained to us about her husband's sexual practices. The doctor hadn't found signs of sexual abuse, but the child had vaginal and anal infections.

'Sexual abuse was confirmed by Dr Higgs. We asked her if she could deal with it in a low-profile way, because we wanted to deal with it in a strategic way. So we said if she did find anything disturbing we would prefer it if she would admit the child to hospital for investigation without saying why and then we'd come along the following day with the other children. The point was we had a plan. But the ancillary worker we'd sent to the hospital rang up and told one of us to get down there quick, the doctor had told the mother she thought the child had been abused and the mother was screaming the place down and she'd nearly strangled the child. She wasn't aware of the suspicions – we were, because we'd been on courses! We wanted to tell the mother gently the next day and work through with her a way to protect the children. The doctor had confronted the mother with it and the mother wanted to strangle the kid – which often happens.

'Dr Higgs was quite certain and wanted to see the other children. We dropped the dad off at the police station. He abhorred the very suggestion that he was a suspect. We were absolutely livid. And worn out. The next day Dr Higgs examined the child again with the police surgeon who at the time confirmed the findings – but later wouldn't be cited as a second opinion and said he'd only been acting on Dr Higgs' direction. The next morning we contacted the police and the sergeant said he refused to investigate; he wouldn't act on another anus unless he got a signed statement from Dr Higgs on his desk.

'Initially the police refused to come round here to the centre. We explained that we had specially set-up rooms and toys, everything needed for this kind of work.' In line with current government thinking – but unfunded by the county council – the Cleveland Family Centre had created a special facility for children to talk. Funds for this had

133

been raised largely through their own initiatives, or through donations made by themselves after giving talks in their own time. The unit had a two-way mirror and plenty of playthings.

'The police said we had to bring the children round to the station one by one. I said, "I refuse". Eventually they agreed to come round here. The child was also quite frightened of men and would you believe it they came round with a policewoman and a great big man – I mean enormous. Then the policewoman said to the child, 'Guess what I do, I'm a policewoman.' Well, this child's father was a burglar, she'd had police officers running through her bedroom at night while her father jumped out of the window. So the most sinister thing in her life was a policeperson. All these children were under five, yet they were expected to talk about their genital areas.

'We'd noticed inappropriate sexual behaviour, and the child had begun to tell us things, like her father touched her down there whenever he wanted to. But when her mother heard her say that, she told her if she ever said that again she'd kill her. So she never did say it again. The big policeman asked one of the kids what kind of sweets he liked and said he'd go and get some for him. He went out and never came back again.'

Arrgghh – the social workers' lament

For the social workers whose job it was to deal on a day-to-day basis with the crisis, the pressure was enormous. One headquarters social worker remembers the beginning.

'At ten to nine the phone rang, I was just putting on my coat to go to work and my colleague told me such-and-such children were all in hospital, they'd been sexually abused. Arrgghh! I knew these children, not with anything approaching abuse in mind, just helping their mum pad

her way through a divorce, new claims at DHSS, rational-
ising the housing situation, ordinary support. And it just
never stopped after that.

'One of the children had been taken to hospital, where
they found anal dilatation signs and hymenal tears, and
similar signs were found on her sisters. We took a place of
safety order, the mother agreed with that. There were no
suspicions voiced except by the mother; the little one was
only two and was with her mother all the time, and there
was only one other person with access to all three. I can
remember sitting in a coffee shop, the mother wringing her
hands and weeping, saying, "I don't want to think it, but
it's either me or him." The police were involved immediately. The police surgeon had seen the children and there
was no medical dispute. The older two were boarded out
to a foster home, mum came with us and gave the children
permission to let Auntie Bloggs look after them. She rang
them every day, she saw them twice a week until the
person the children said was the perpetrator was arrested.

'A policewoman and I did the disclosure work together,
very constructively, and mum was present. One of the little
girls said she had a secret. A few days later we established
with this little girl that we all knew what safe meant: she
decided you were safe when nothing nasty could happen to
you and she was safe crossing the road with you or the lol-
lipop lady. I got a picture of a child who was quite clear
about where and with whom she was and wasn't safe.
What about such-and-such a house? 'No.' We were puzzled
about what on earth it could be that she wasn't kept safe
from. She gave a big sigh and said, "Getting a sore bum
and tuppence, silly!" In much the same way we established
who it was. How did it happen, we wondered. Again she
slapped her hand on the table and said, "Don't be silly,
you know it's only such-and-such can do things like that!"

So we said just to make sure could the policewoman write it down and we'll read it back?

'She was very fond of the perpetrator – no negative feelings, except that he'd left them. It was their father.

'I felt quite sorry for the policewoman, because she'd got the statement, and took it back to the station hoping to be able to pick him up on that, but probably wisely – I was indignant at the time, but having run a few cases through the courts subsequently they may have been right – they were waiting for the older child to disclose, too. My feeling was that there were kids here who could go home right away if he was off the street. We'd gone for the interim care order, so that they could go home, and in case he got bail we could lift them. The mother was fully in agreement. She's often said she was very grateful for the diagnosis and to us, because it took matters out of her hands, it took decisions for her while she got straightened out.

'All the time there have been all the complaints about lack of police co-operation, but it doesn't seem to have been so down at the sharp end, and I've had that in my other cases, too. Having said that, I was aware that the police were getting different pressures than we were – were very frustrated, and more feelings of doubt were passed down to them from above than they had themselves. Conversations with people you'd worked with for six years became stilted.

'The CID officers dealing with this case were absolutely convinced. But there was a genuine feeling that it had to be watertight. One thing that made me quite cross later was when somebody said, "These children have been *subjected* to divulgence interviews," and I thought what do they think we do to these kids, pin them up by the thumbs against the wall? The reason it takes time is because it takes time getting to know people. The children didn't know the police people, they had no real grounds to trust any of us, and some children were of an age to know what they were saying, that there would be consequences. But these interviews were interspersed with conversations about Care Bears and Brownies. People think social workers are well-meaning duffers, and that's offended me enormously.

'In another case a mother rang us for advice because her two-year-old had told her something. We made arrangements to go out and see her and because she was saying she'd got to know if the child had been damaged, we suggested she could see a doctor. So she took the child to see Dr Higgs. She had hymenal tears. We weren't expecting to get any statement from the two-year-old, obviously, but she was a particularly bright child and I asked the policewoman whether she honestly thought anything the child said could be used in evidence. She thought not, but we needed to have as much idea as possible when she faced the perpetrator, who was 17. So we abandoned evidential work aimed at a prosecution, and asked the child to show us what she'd called the boy's rude game, and she did. The work there was to reassure the mother that the little girl wasn't ruined for life. It was a close and sensible family, and you could see they'd deal with it calmly when they'd finished being angry about it. He was questioned, denied it absolutely and left the area. The physical evidence wouldn't stand up in court as corroboration.'

The controversy transformed the evidential criteria required of social workers. Where once disclosure – a clear statement by a child that it had been abused – armed with physical signs might have been watertight, now neither seemed to be sufficient.

'I find that very difficult,' said this social worker. 'I can see why, but I cannot believe there's never been anybody arrested for abusing a two-year-old when they've denied it. At one time we used to have disclosures, the person would utterly deny, even though the child was bitterly saying it happened. We would seek medical evidence because that would be the only thing that would make a difference. But now we've got the medical evidence and it isn't enough. In the present atmosphere disclosure work is coming under fire, too. They say you're looking for it and you knew what you wanted the child to say.'

Suspicions surrounding the disclosure work reached such a point during the Cleveland inquiry that many of the constraints imposed by the judiciary, once children had been made wards of court, effectively banned any further disclosure work – either to gather evidence or to provide therapy for the child.

Another social worker posted at a rural area office found the same constraints. A boy of eleven and his four-year-old sister were referred to her by the boy's school. There were physical signs suggesting abuse on both children and she began working with them to build trust. 'The boy would tell anybody. He was abusing other children, and he went on to make allegations not only about school but also about what had happened between him and his stepfather at home, and that he'd abused his sister. I'd only intended to build up a relationship, and all this was hurled at me. It took a lot longer with the little girl. She was very frightened, she clung to adults and eventually established a good relationship with the foster parents we placed her with, and felt able to describe what her stepfather had done to her brother, and to her, saying things like, "My daddy's got a big cock." It was anal abuse in both, and vaginal signs in the girl. There was complete denial from the parents. The father was very organised and involved in the parents' support group. He was very intelligent, mum was totally dominated by the stepfather and didn't say anything at all.

'I wasn't able to do any work with this family. We had many threats from the stepfather. And he threatened the children about speaking to me. The parents immediately asked for another opinion, so the case went before the second opinion panel, which actually supported the diagnosis, and also concluded that they had been physically and emotionally abused. The little girl couldn't play or feed herself. The boy was causing tremendous problems in the children's home, trying to abuse younger children, leaving dirty messages around to female members of staff, going to newsagents and taking pictures of women out of the Sun, putting them in his underpants and socks and pinning them up in the children's home. The staff felt unable to cope with him.

'The allegations were put to the stepfather, who denied them. Then the parents initiated wardship proceedings, which we didn't oppose. They were made wards of court, which gave the parents access. The kids didn't request any contact with the parents, and when they had contact the little girl, who had settled down, would shake uncontrollably, wander about during the night, find any food she could lay her hands on, wet the bed. After one visit she was up all night, it was dreadful, screaming, "Don't let me go back home."

'The daughter retracted her statements during one of those visits, with a social worker present. The stepfather mentioned in access visits that he was involved in the parents' group and asked about other children.

'The first access was traumatic. It consisted of an interrogation by the stepfather of the boy: "Don't you make me go to prison, your mam will die because of all this." This was the first contact they'd had for months: the boy was just sobbing and after 15 minutes retracted all his previous statements, which was expected. The stepfather went when he got the retraction, leaving the children in a trembling state. We later found out that he'd audiotaped the access visit, so he had recorded retraction on tape. The next visit was a complete reverse – loving man, presents for the children – but very little was said. The little girl sat in silence, she brought her packed lunch, ate it and then wanted to leave. The visits have gone on like that.

'The police felt they did not have a case after they did an initial investigation, because of the age of the younger child and the mental state of the older child. But the police have never to this day spoken to the little girl. In the wardship hearing, disclosure work was halted. There was a blanket direction in most of the cases that we couldn't do disclosure work. One of our advantages in this case was that I had already been doing it. But I wasn't able to offer any further treatment for the little girl. She did well with her foster parents – she'd compare her life there with her life at home, and ask them things like, "Why do you play with me?" It's about re-parenting and re-learning now.

'We discovered that the stepfather had further offences – that was another thing. The police would normally come to a case conference with that information, but they'd been under pressure themselves. The information was passed to me totally out of the blue by the solicitor who'd represented the man before and purely by chance bumped into me in court. He whispered in my ear that there had been an indecent assault on an eight-year-old girl a few years ago. When I rang the police with the information they were taken aback, so it was genuine overwork. This would have been in late June, after things had degenerated. But our relations were quite good and the decision not to take the matter any further was because they thought it wouldn't stand up in court.'

This case was one of the few that ultimately went according to Cleveland County Council's recommendations. The little girl remained with her foster parents who were considering adopting. No access was ever again granted by the High Court judge who settled her affairs in January 1988. The boy was returned to a special residential school and boarded in a residential home at weekends. The little girl was apparently overjoyed; the boy was left with his sorrows. 'After all,' said the social worker, sadly, 'his relationship with his stepfather was the only relationship he'd ever known. He'll need a lot of help right into his adulthood.'

Cleveland social workers are allocated points according to their cases and these points are designed to control their workload. This social worker's load went way over the scale during the crisis. Yet still she had to have what amounted to two whole days a week ferrying a little boy to access visits to his stepfather and grandparents, to his mother, and to his biological father. 'The court ordered access for all the parties. That meant three times a week. Picking the child up could take me half a day, so for each party that was one and a half days out of my week; he also had play therapy, so that was two days on this one kid. But when we went to court, of course, the media weren't interested in that – they scuttled out when they heard we were recommending that he go to live with his father.'

'A forgiving lot'

By the end of May some 60 children suspected of having been sexually abused were in the council's care. It was wild. 'In our office it got to be a joke. "It just can't be another case," we'd say, but it was,' recalled a worker on the outskirts of Middlesbrough. Her own workload had gone way beyond the scale. 'People were totally shocked, they felt it was unreal. You'd be dashing here, dashing there, settling children in somewhere, organising case conferences, it took up all your time. All the routine things weren't being done. Any work I had with other clients just went. Child protection work became the most important, so other cases were just blowing because we didn't have time to deal with them.'

A city centre social worker remembered that even before the crisis, 'My team was already struggling. It seemed as if the golden oldies were dropping off. I was already dealing with five cases, including a particularly difficult one – a classic, following the pattern of disclosure, denial, chaos, suppression, retraction. Before it all started I actually said to somebody, "Look, I don't know about everybody else but I'm not waving, I'm drowning here." We were talking about staff not being replaced, empty desks, we were off doing one-off visits to keep people ticking over. I had a conversation about this being the sort of atmosphere and circumstances in which something dreadful could happen. Like the Jasmine Beckford case. Nerve-racking.'

Case workers had little sense yet that their individual crisis was historic. 'People felt they hadn't been supported by management. You felt you were on your own and if you didn't cover your back nobody else would,' said one senior staffer. 'Management could have given more information, they could have sent somebody out on a weekly basis to tell us what was happening. All the information we got was in the media, we were just picking up snippets, general gossip. I went to one meeting, and that had been called by social workers for social workers to give support. It was really nice. There was high turnover and no strategy. People got angry. The crisis didn't bring social workers together, it separated them, they didn't have the time to consult colleagues. I felt very isolated, because I was making decisions alone when it was normally a sharing process. But all that went because people were in and out and never at their desks.'

A rank-and-filer at headquarters remembers the long hours. 'I never got home in time for "Coronation Street", it would usually be about nine o'clock by the time I got in. Then there was the exhaustion. I screamed a lot, wept a lot, threw up a lot. And I was very angry. Publicly the county probably did a good job, but we missed most of it because while they were on "Nationwide" we were out there. There were areas of tactlessness: they were slow coming round with messages of support and people were hearing things in the press before we heard it from the department. People felt bitter about that. But being a forgiving lot we just got on with it. We were all struggling individually without realising it was going on all over the county. I don't think anybody at lower levels was aware of the strategic implications being shared. That might have made a difference. Instead, each team was probably thinking they were sinking. It would have been less debilitating to have known that we were part of a more important struggle.'

Like the nurses at Middlesbrough General Hospital, like some of the police, like the health visitors, the rank-and-file social workers were cast in the role of the hired hands: they were the *workers* who were not consulted by the bosses, and so while they were in the middle of making history, they were not invited to help make the strategy for the future.

Increasingly, too, some social workers found themselves politically as well as professionally besieged. Child sex abuse was, quite correctly, perceived by people opposed to the diagnosis as no longer belonging to a populist politics of hanging and flogging but to a politics with a critique of patriarchy and power in the family. Some social workers say they were interrogated by defence lawyers in court not only about which doctor had examined the children in care, but about their own personal lives and their politics. 'It's very personal. They'll ask you in court, how you stand politically about the present situation – they never did before. I've never been asked about my personal life, my family, which party I'm a member of. I've actually been asked, "Are you married?" That's never cropped up previously,' said one social worker.

Political allegiance did not explain the social services staff's readiness to trust the anal dilatation diagnosis: many social workers shared a disposition to disbelieve the scale of abuse. But nursing officer Marjorie Dunn explained that social workers were for the first time being presented with strong medical evidence. 'It was so rare for doctors to make a positive diagnosis, so when you did get one very suggestive of sexual abuse – and that's all Dr Higgs really said – then people acted on it with confidence. It was all a matter of confidence, because they felt they were acting on genuine information.'

A senior social worker in one of the area offices which had the stamina to cope with a large swathe of referrals, and to nurture a viable relationship with the police well into the crisis, also reckoned that social workers' history with physical neglect and abuse informed their attitude to medical evidence:

'We used physical abuse as a model. We've got more and more comfortable coping with that, and that relied very much on medical diagnosis. Over the past ten years we have come to respect police methods: some officers were more used to interviewing people with a view to getting at the facts, whereas we are good at gaining impressions. Thoughtlessly – we just didn't think about it – sexual abuse was regarded in the same light. In a way that was right, but it is a more secret process and demands far more co-operation and subtlety, precisely because of the secrecy and the threats to children. The key to physical abuse was always the initial diagnosis, so we operated in the same way. So what knocked the shit out of us was the discovery that this key aspect was kicked from under us by the police surgeon. We started to regard the initial finding as needing further investigation rather than as evidence of sexual abuse. We still had the police coming to case conferences, but we only ever heard, "We are continuing investigations." They continued and continued and continued and never seemed to get anywhere. Disbelief was pinned on the police surgeon, Dr Irvine. At grassroots level, relationships with the police continued to be good and there was no real conflict, although formally they continued to investigate and informally they didn't believe the paediatricians. We were arguing about something beyond our realm. In the same way as we worked with physical abuse and neglect, we always looked at the possible alternatives, we looked very carefully, and yet at the end of the day we were always faced with a strong diagnosis and a whole range of statements or behaviour.'

This social worker's busy area office was based in a working-class community, and he believed that the high density of referrals in some areas like his reflected the way their economic deprivation produced not greater levels of sexual abuse but greater exposure to all kinds of social service scrutiny. But when abuse was suspected in 'the "nice" families, the families of teachers, middle-class people, foster families who had gone through intensive scrutiny and come out of it with nine out of ten, then that made people wonder, how can you tell? We had to distrust everything we knew. We could disbelieve the suspicion, and my god we wanted to. But we didn't, because if we ignored the evidence that sexual abuse is an under-discovered activity, then it would have been like being presented with two different diagnoses and accepting the no-abuse option because it was easier. A lot of us found it very difficult to deal with, but we made conscious decisions not to make judgements based on gut reactions, like "Oh no, they can't be!" We overcame that by looking coldly at it. I don't think the police took that further step.

'Our difficulty was that we had no resources except ourselves. The whole thing became centred on the diagnosis. The police failure was not just to do with attitudes but with resources; like in all the agencies, everybody was running around like blue-arsed flies. But social services became marooned in this drama because the police abstained.'

Losing in the courts

As May ran into June, the Cleveland County Council began to have legal difficulties. The council usually went to the juvenile court to seek an interim care order, which gave it the power to intervene in a family and to plan protection for the children. But as anal dilatation began to be contested as a diagnosis, the council began losing in the juvenile courts and resorted to wardship proceedings in the High Court. Wardship lightened the council's load because it took over protection planning: once children became wards of court, they came under the court's jurisdiction. Furthermore, there was a formidable waiting list in the juvenile court and a severe shortage of guardians who could be appointed as independent representatives of the children. Local lawyers representing families contesting the diagnosis met with the county management and agreed to go for wardship.

One council officer recalled that a pattern began to

emerge in the juvenile courts that interim orders would be granted only if, 'Apart from the diagnosis, other things were worrying. It was filtering back to us that some judges were approaching the matter on the basis that unless medical evidence, on a high standard of proof, could stand up, then further investigation was thereby flawed. If cause for concern *is* detected, and it increasingly emerged that anal dilatation, for example, *is* seen as a cause for concern, then we needed a *mandate* to investigate further. We were not getting that mandate from the courts.'

By early June Dr Paul and Dr Roberts had been up in Cleveland challenging the anal dilatation diagnosis. They were powerful and persuasive witnesses – the courts became afraid of keeping children away from their homes. One county officer reckoned that the courts weren't so much rejecting the diagnosis offered by Dr Higgs and Dr Wyatt as saying they wouldn't keep children in care. The political atmosphere no doubt infected the courts, too. In one juvenile case, nearly 20 members of the press crowded into the court to hear the magistrate refuse an interim order. Speculation circulated around the courthouse at the time that the court had backed off. But from what – from being seen to be breaking up families? Or protecting children against their fathers? Or from taking responsibility for something society had historically turned its back on?

That caution spread when the council turned to the High Court and wardship. The message coming from the courts seemed to be: no go. Cleveland lost the ability not only to keep some of the children in care, but also to continue their inquiries and to do disclosure or therapeutic interviews with the children they feared were at risk. Either way, the courts seemed to be complicit in the campaign to bury sexual abuse. In some cases the children could no longer be medically monitored in any case, because that would have required leave of the court. 'And no way would the parents let Dr Higgs or Dr Wyatt see the children ever again, and no way was the judge going to order it,' said a senior social worker.

There was also a blanket embargo on the settlements in the wardship cases. When children were returned home, no information was given to the public about the terms, about continued medical monitoring or social services supervision. Not surprisingly, the media reported that children had been 'released' without being able to report that in many cases they were being released into protective packages agreed between the court, social services and the parents – and those protective packages meant that, if the biological father was the suspected perpetrator, he must leave the home. The effect of the embargo was disastrous: the county council was thereafter to lose the propaganda battle. It couldn't reveal or comment upon the frequently complex arrangements being made, with its agreement, to get children back home. Nor could it communicate the impact of the ban on disclosure work: the county had been presented with 'cause for concern' but was not allowed to find out from the children themselves what was in their minds.

The effect of these silences was to concede the argument to the campaign against the council and the doctors. It also seems to have stilled the council when it needed perhaps to speak out. Debates raged within the corridors of Marton House about whether the department should refute some of the attacks made by some of the parents. In one case, a social worker was reported in the press in autumn 1987 as having struck a client and then taken her baby from her. Stuart Bell was reported in the *Evening Gazette* on 13 October as saying, 'There is an attitude of mind within Cleveland social services which is positively detrimental to mothers and children and this attitude really has to be purged.' One camp in the department wanted to reveal the history of its relationship with this rather violent woman; the other felt bound by the ethics of confidentiality – that the woman was entitled to have her privacy protected. When the case came to court in March 1988 it was clearly not one of the 'Cleveland crisis' cases. The mother's five other children were already in care – she had previously swapped one of them for an alsatian dog. The social worker had arrived after a fracas, with no thought of care orders. After another skirmish the child was taken into care – an order that was later confirmed by the High Court. The social worker was exonerated and the mother convicted of criminal damage. Months later, the social worker said he was still waiting for an apology from Mr Bell.

After the May Bank Holiday the social services were not only running out of facilities but they were also exhausting the labour time of their own staff. Parents, in particular, weren't getting social work attention, and many of them felt they were being treated briskly, at best. 'The result was that the parents turned to each other,' said a social worker. 'The other unfortunate consequence was that they understandably regarded themselves as prime suspects when no social worker would have approached parents on that basis.'

The crisis of accommodation and treatment resources compounded the parents' distress. In one case part of a local detention centre was made available for some of the children: there could have been no clearer message that they were being punished. Here was a community which, literally, could not guarantee children's safety.

Emergency measures

Crash courses were quickly organised when the council called in Madge Bray, one of the country's most

149

experienced sexual abuse consultants, who had worked with around 100 cases of sexual abuse before being drafted into Cleveland. The county council also set up a special Children's Resource Centre in June in a temporary block near to Middlesbrough General's children's ward, directed by Deborah Glassbrook, an experienced worker with sexually abused children who had worked with the national ChildLine.

For some social workers the pressure of the crisis, and its prelude – the general criticism bearing down on social workers for failure to intervene quickly or dramatically enough – haunted their consciences and produced over-reaction. In one widely publicised case, a social worker regarded by her colleagues as a sensitive woman found herself conducting unusually heavy interviews with children suspected of having been abused. When tapes of videoed interviews were demanded as evidence in a wardship hearing, she began to be alarmed that she had pushed the children too hard, and erased some of the interview. In her panic at her own reaction she became seriously distressed and disappeared. Excerpts from tapes were shown on a nationally networked television programme after the Butler-Sloss report was published, as an example of the pressure to which children had been subjected – although the programme did not comment on police interviews which had also provoked social services protests. In retrospect, the social worker's practices expressed the state of thinking in some quarters that the pressure on children to deny any abuse had to be matched by equally strong control by child protection workers – a view which is now discredited. But more than that, the social worker's disposition was also informed by her experience. She had been responsible for a family in which the father had previous convictions for indecency. Although the social

worker was working with the family, she was persuaded by
the mother to endorse the father's being united with his
family, and only later, after a family fracas, learned from
the children that they had been subjected to bizarre, sadis-
tic behaviour by the father. Aware that she had not been
vigilant enough, she was anxious not to make the same
mistake again.

Madge Bray operated from her own consultancy, the
Sexual Abuse Child Consultant Service, set up because
she was frustrated at the lack of any appropriate space for
therapeutic disclosure work within local authorities, with
whom she preferred to work. A successful advocate for
children in the courts, she was much admired in social
service departments and police authorities which called
in her expertise. She clarified her own objectives when,
during the judicial inquiry, she was questioned about the
risk of putting undue pressure on children to 'confess'.
She did not pressurise children. 'I switch off my own need
to know,' she explained, insisting, as did other professionals skilled in helping children unburden themselves, that
children had to be encouraged to talk in their own way and
in their own time. In Cleveland she found disbelief, impot-
ence and 'an appalling lack of facilities'.

Under stiff cross-examination at the inquiry, Director of
Social Services Mike Bishop explained that 'at the height
of the crisis we did not have the resources to do the investigations that we do now and which I regard as good
practice'. Pressed about his management methods and
whether he should not have 'trimmed the course a little',
he cited the resource centre as an example of exactly that.
From the beginning of June, 'it took us a month to get
those management methods in operation. We got the children's resource centre. We found the money to do it, we
found the staff, we found the premises, and it was set up in

four weeks. That, with respect, is *moving*, in local authority terms.'

Debbie Glassbrook walked into a situation in which no one was equipped to deal with the deluge, and in which the county desperately needed corroboration from children if it was to defend its positive response to the diagnosis and protect the children it had taken into its trusteeship. Some social workers or therapists might have felt compelled to hurry the process, not least because the skids were under the county council. But she too insisted that 'children only disclose if they're ready to. And you can help it get ready by making it feel safe and confident. Sexual abuse is a process of sexualisation, it is not like rape; it is an ongoing sexual and emotional relationship. Sexual abuse isn't about sex, it is about power and control and the way we learn about that in this society. The expectation of males and females is about power. One of the ways we learn about power is through sexuality. The feelings are wrapped up inside the children. And what they're not in touch with is the confusing messages from outside. A lot of abused children feel bad and dirty inside, so the medical examination is part of the therapeutic process because we can show them that we can make it better and affirm the child's body. A lot of older children feel they've got cancer inside, that something has invaded them, and so a medical examination can help clear that away.

'We need a place of safety because we have to undo all the work done by the offender. You must take responsibility *from* the child. We are all justifying our own anger and anguish. We've been allowing kids to go on taking our pain and anxiety. The police say we must protect children, we must try to get the offender. Our point of view is that we often can't remove the offender and that's why we need police co-operation. But I don't think England is ready yet to have a therapeutic response to offenders. In the United States there tends to be a care and control response to the offender, whereas here it is still "get the bastard and cut his balls off" or stick him in jail. England is still too tied up in the Empire and the "shoot the buggers" approach. But often the offenders have been abused and prison reinforces the abuse.'

What distinguished Debbie Glassbrook and her colleagues from earlier traditions of 'social purity' which were active during the late nineteenth and early twentieth centuries, and which were instrumental in encouraging legislation against the sexual exploitation of children, was that the modernists were not crusading for chastity nor denying the sexuality of children themselves, by representing them as de-sexualised innocents polluted by corrupt adult desire. 'Society denies children their own sexuality, it gives negative messages to children about their bodies.' For them the issue was not about mythologising some imagined state of sexual innocence, but exposing the prevalence of predatory raids on the sexual autonomy of children. 'Sexual abuse is not an altruistic touch, it is intended to gratify an adult's need. All of us can cuddle kids and get satisfaction from that, and to say we can't cuddle any more is failing to understand the boundaries, and that's because they're not clear about their own sexuality,' said Debbie Glassbrook.

During the summer of 1987 disclosure work like that done by Debbie Glassbrook's centre and Madge Bray's consultancy, as well as the evidential conversations between children and social workers, attracted the same onslaught as the diagnosis. Glassbrook defended disclosure work, but distanced herself from an approach adopted by some psychologists, based on the theory that given the weight of pressure not to tell, therapists should consider an equally strong context of security sufficient to encourage disclosure. 'I am determined I am not going to use a child. These children have been through enough. I'm not going to further abuse them to gratify anybody's needs other than their own,' she said.

So-called disclosure work was fiercely contested during the months of May and June, perhaps because the prospect of children sharing the secrets of their families with strangers seemed an offence against the sanctity of the family and the historically protected privacy of parents. It was as if children talking was deemed an act of treachery. The institutional complicity in defending parental power was suggested in the difficulties encountered by child psychologist Heather Bacon in securing either therapeutic collaboration or the sharing of resources by the county's child and adolescent psychiatry units in the North and South Tees health districts. She had been unable in the two years she had worked in Cleveland before the crisis to persuade child psychiatrist Dr Chisholm to make facilities available for her work in his hospital, or to open up his referral system so that she – or anyone else – could refer children in need of help directly to him. This was standard practice in some other health authorities. He was reluctant to work on sexual abuse as such, and did not agree with her approach, which aimed to expand perception of the problem beyond the individual pathology of the child and to investigate the systems of power operating within families. Her approach implied that the problem originated not in the child but in power within the family, while his approach implied that children, not families, or structures of power, were the problem.

The politics of this debate was mostly suppressed during the long months of the inquiry. Venerable psychiatrists descended from the Establishment to engage in semantic tournaments about the efficacy of 'diagnostic' or 'investigative' therapy, to defend or decry both the means and the ends of encouraging children to talk. At the end of the inquiry, the Official Solicitor, whose department has national responsibility for children in care, no doubt echoed the feeling among most social workers and therapists, that 'children feel safe if they experience safety', but expressed the Establishment's distaste for disclosure work, representing it as 'dangerous' because it 'presupposes' that abuse has taken place. The fact was that in Cleveland the diagnosis was the dominant source of suspicion: disclosure was only its accomplice. No debate was allowed about the implications for childcare, about the encirclement of children in atomised nuclear families, or about a society which provides little sanctuary for children other than 'children's homes', asylums which are known to expose children to yet more abuse.

The theory and the practice: social work and the family

But the implications of all this were not lost on social workers, whose professional premises were being shaken to the roots by the new consciousness of sexual abuse. In Cleveland they hardly had the time to make sense of it all before they were besieged. But in Leeds, for example, social work planners, paediatricians, police and psychologists had matched the mounting demand on their services by a long process of consciousness-raising among themselves. It was this that clarified for them what exactly was at stake, and what they were up against.

Jill McMurray, who co-ordinated the city's register of children at risk during this time, recalls a tragic case which alerted her colleagues to the dilemma: to intervene or not to intervene. Fourteen-year-old Jane Olkiewicz was murdered in 1985 by her stepfather, who had been sexually abusing her for some years. The girl had disclosed that she was being sexually abused to her mother, and to her father. Social services took no action after being reassured by the girl's committed, caring mother that the child was being protected. The stepfather killed the girl, his wife and himself. 'That case helped us to realise that when a child has disclosed, we mustn't just leave it to a parent to take responsibility – some parents are furious about that, but we learned a lot from that case.' That didn't mean taking the child into care, but neither did it mean leaving the whole burden of responsibility on a parent.

What the re-discovery of sexual abuse also taught Jill McMurray was that she had to re-think her whole history as a social worker. By now a childcare manager, she reckoned that if she had still been in direct contact with families it would all have been more difficult, 'because I would have said, "No, it can't be *this* family! Because I know them!" I've worked with children and with "maladjusted" children, and for me there was always something missing – the theoretical base never seemed quite right. There was always a missing something. Sexual abuse is the missing something. A lot of children express their pain through being very withdrawn or angry or violent. I felt dreadful guilt about the number of children I'd tried to help by getting them to fit in better at home, children who were telling me, "But I hate him! I don't want to go home." We never had the answer. We had never asked: why? We never had an explanation, because the jigsaw had a piece missing. If people are stuck at the point of saying "it can't be happening" then sometimes they collude with the family. Social workers have been trained to keep families together, to find the best in people and get the best out of people.'

Her experience confirms recent reflections on the shifts in social policy over the last century. Linda Gordon's germinal study of the history of family violence and its survivors, *Heroes of Their Own Lives*,[2] re-thinks the genesis of the modern welfare state and child protection agencies. She argues that the main structures mirrored the very movements which had created them, ranging from feminism to social purity politics. They had campaigned against brutality, domestic depravity and the sexual molestation of children on the one hand, and on the other, the problem of the perpetrators – men. After the first decade or so of the twentieth century the focus on the family became blurred, particularly with the demise of the first wave of feminism. Instead, sexual abuse was deemed to be not so much a problem of the family as something to fear from strangers. The victims were also re-defined, according to Gordon, whose evidence from Boston's social service records challenges the notion of children's passive complicity. There was 'widespread and energetic resistance' by children, albeit 'confused, varied and unsteady'. Professionals did not so much ignore these children's cries for help as re-interpret them: delinquency was discovered. The assailant, too, was redefined: he was no longer a family man but a stranger. 'Both re-definitions served to withdraw scrutiny from family relationships and from what might be the cultural and social sources of this exclusively male crime.'

For sure, what the carefully crafted approach of Jill McMurray and the bitterly contested efforts of Cleveland social services revealed was that the new consciousness of child sexual abuse was bringing it all back home again to fathers and the family.

The men's movement

What made the Cleveland case so remarkable was not so much the number of referrals as the mass dissent from the diagnosis. Not in 100 years had patriarchal society been so profoundly and publicly confronted by the scale of men's sexual abuse of children. Male sexuality was the problem, but in the great sex scandal of the 1980s that had become almost the unsayable.

During the early months of the summer, individual resistance became collective revolt. Yet although the rebellion became known for the hostility to Dr Higgs and Dr Wyatt, not all fathers and their families who became involved in the revolt began by disbelieving the diagnosis. In one household which joined up with the Parents Support Group formed during the summer, both parents were ready to contemplate the possibility that their toddler had been abused. She had been seen by a paediatrician who diagnosed anal dilatation, and within a few days was taken into foster care. The family were told by a social worker that they had to assume that sexual abuse had taken place. The family secured a second opinion from Dr Raine Roberts, who rejected the diagnosis.

The family and social services worked out a 'protection package', an arrangement agreed by all that the child would not see her father and would be cared for temporarily by her mother and her aunt. Dr Wyatt, however, rigidly refused to accept the package. It appeared to the family that he would not sanction any protection package that the family could have offered. It was this that began to make them feel imprisoned by the diagnosis and the doctors.

'Sue Richardson wanted to be more flexible, and she accepted our package. She doesn't seem to have had the line that the diagnosis was infallible,' said a relative. 'We were prepared to co-operate. But I don't believe it when social services said it wasn't true that children were taken into care on the basis of the diagnosis alone – they just weren't resourced to assess the child.

'That left us in the worst position, which was that there would be no [named] abuser. That was our nightmare. And I think it was that kind of thing that led to the desperation of the parents who contested the diagnosis. It has to be acknowledged that in some way the diagnosis might be wrong and that the most important work is with the child. If that had been the case we would have been all right, because we would have helped in every way.'

This family also enjoyed the support of their social worker. 'She responded to us very well. That worried me, because we're middle class, we're articulate and we complained to everybody. I worried about the more powerless people.'

Not all the middle-class families were so privileged. In one case no one from social services engaged with the mother. For months she was marooned, separated from her children, and briefly from her husband, too.

A Cleveland county council officer reckoned that it was in the absence of adequate social services support that 'the parents naturally turned towards each other'.

Once rumours of a swathe of care orders resulting from the diagnosis began circulating around the courts, local lawyers, well known in Middlesbrough for their combative defence of their clients – whether 'rough' or 'respectable' – intervened. According to one solicitor, 'The difficulty was that the local authority didn't seem to consider an alternative explanation [for the medical diagnosis]. Then as the rumblings got louder, certain social services people came to accept that there may be an alternative explanation, and the ground shifted totally.' Second opinions were sought, and by mid-June resistance was being organised. Lawyers were galvanised, not only in representing fathers who felt accused, but positively in the public debate. They now had the opportunity to canvass for clients and this enabled local solicitors to make it known where fathers would find help.

At this point the geography of Ward 9, the sprawling location where many children suspected of being sexually abused were living, became crucial. And as the numbers grew to crisis proportions over the weekend of 13–14 June, nursing staff had to re-organise the accommodation. Families were crowded into a set of cubicles on the ward, but soon they too were filled. Relocation of these children and their families created the conditions for the parents' revolt.

Nursing staff reckoned that a spatial solution to the mayhem might be to put all hospitalised cases of sexual abuse, together with their families, into an enclave known as Ward 2 at the end of the main Ward 9. 'The nurses were so fed up that they put them all in there. I don't know that it was a good idea – because it meant that the parents got together,' said one of the nurses.

A county council worker recalled that, 'By chance I went to Middlesbrough General to see a social worker. I was told she was on the ward. I went over to find her talking to four sets of parents, all together, where one vociferous gentleman was just winding her up, saying, "You're telling us we've been abusing our children!"'

The nurses felt both helpless and blameless, yet they were being shouted at and even spat at by both parents and children. 'That was what the nurses found so hard – being treated to such aggression by the families. Parents would egg on the children. There was a friend of one of the families, he was always wanting to organise the press and television. He visited daily,' said one nurse. 'All those parents and children screaming. He was a catalyst, he had quite a hidden power about him; you treated him very carefully. He was there every day and I got the feeling that the parents were frightened of him. He called the tune. One family wanted to say something publicly supportive of Dr Higgs and Dr Wyatt, but were frightened because of what might happen. So they said to a group of us, "We're grateful for Dr Wyatt bringing this to light."

'There was another side. Although it was all an administrative and medical mess, there was a feeling that the situation was being used for financial gain – people got money for getting their story in the papers, as well as a lot of public sympathy. The tabloids especially were violently against Dr Higgs and Dr Wyatt and the real issue was lost – sexual abuse of children for adult gratification. Making more fuss was the thing. The wider implications didn't get through.'

It was that June weekend which brought the Rev Michael Wright into the drama. He was contacted by a member of his congregation who asked him to help a neighbour whose three children had been put under a Place of Safety Order after a sexual abuse diagnosis by Dr Higgs. When he visited the couple, he said, 'I found not what I'd expected, frankly. I'd expected I'd find a certain sort of tension between the two of them, the mother falling out with the father. I thought if the children had been abused it was likely to be the father, and there would be some suspicion between them, with somebody vehemently denying it. What I found was a young and very capable couple and they had an ability to describe their experiences in careful detail. Their three children were among 19 taken into care in the same outpatients clinic on 13 June. I'd got parents who were frightened of taking their children back to hospital, frightened of other children, frightened of other tensions, because of the suspicions of someone in the family. There's an insidious suspicion. It's very difficult because the parents deny and the children deny. So you've got to be a smart cookie to get at the truth.'

He believed that it wasn't until the parents got press publicity that social services agreed to second opinions and then to an independent panel of six doctors to provide second opinions.

'My role was to reflect the views of parents,' explained the Rev Wright. 'I went to John Urch, secretary of the Community Health Council, who'd been up to his neck in it all for five weeks, and who said that various people were very concerned, including senior police officers, the district manager of the health authority, senior nurses, the clerk to the court.' John Urch put Wright in touch with another group of parents who had been meeting together, and continued to point angry parents his way. Like Rev Wright, John Urch felt that his 'community' responsibility was to the fathers. Together they helped organise a Parents Support Group. The Rev Wright felt 'impelled to put an advertisement in the paper' in June. A meeting was called, a strategy was planned and on 21 June he wrote to the Tory MP Tim Devlin and Labour MP Stuart Bell, who responded immediately.

Middlesbrough's MP was an ambitious local lad who had been elected for Labour, and although solidly with the right, he had encountered no significant opposition from the left. But by 1983, when a left winger assumed leadership of the city council after many councillors had been de-selected, Bell began to be seen to be consolidating his right-wing base against any possible threat. Bell relied heavily on the block vote mobilised at the local party's

General Management Committee by the General and Municipal Union, which has dominated Tyneside and Teesside Labourism for longer than many an activist cares to remember. It was the favours of these union delegates that he called on at a GMC meeting in July 1987, at which child sexual abuse was to be discussed.

By 1987 he was Labour's number two spokesperson on Ireland, but when the child sexual abuse crisis broke he resigned the post to concentrate more fully on an issue which, he thought, had until then been seen as a prerogative of the left. What began as a populist – and apparently popular – campaign may, however, have marked the end of his ambitions to become a shadow cabinet member and ultimately a Minister. Isolated from other Labour MPs representing neighbouring constituencies, in the House of Commons Bell came to depend on an alliance with Tories. Ironically, some Tory women members of the county council's social services committee did not share his critique of the crisis in Cleveland. He should not have been surprised. Many Tory women adhere to their party's family ideology not so much to defend the power of fathers as to affirm the rights and responsibilities of mothers. In the Tory women's tradition, fear of men – and especially of men's sexual raids on women and children – animated their role as the vanguard of the law and order lobby. By the autumn, Stuart Bell's estrangement from his party's new sexual politics was consummated by a resolution passed by the party conference supporting measures to protect children from sexual abuse. Nonetheless, the stamina of 'sexual Toryism' in the Labour Party was exemplified when Stuart Bell sent in his evidence to the inquiry: he attached a supportive covering note from Labour's deputy leader, Roy Hattersley.

Bell collected a dossier of cases, was in close contact

with the police and with parents, and told the inquiry – at the same time as he modestly denied that he was claiming credit – that the government ordered the inquiry as a result of his campaign. And when he finally appeared before the inquiry, on its final day in December, he repeated his condemnation of Dr Higgs and her diagnosis, and reiterated the Higgs–Richardson conspiracy theory. He also refused to withdraw his allegation, made in a document accompanying the dossier he sent to Health Minister Tony Newton, that councillors Bob Pitt and John Bell had been 'put up' by the social services department to back its expansionist designs by successfully recommending extra funds. It all smacked of sinister machiavellian manoeuvres, he implied, and was supported by his complaint that the department had improperly briefed backbench councillors. In fact the department had addressed all the members of the committee at its June meeting. But Stuart Bell seemed reluctant to believe that the councillors were capable of thinking their own thoughts and making their own proposals to support a department which was carrying out their agreed project – to make child abuse its priority.

Stuart Bell adopted an uncompromising stance throughout 1987. Parents, he said, had been falsely accused. Cross-examined, however, by Dr Higgs' counsel, Robert Nelson, QC, the profile of the 17 groups of parents he had been defending looked shadier than he had led the public to believe. With time running out on the final afternoon, Mr Nelson got through the first five cases represented by Mr Bell before the judge stopped him – all of them had shown signs ranging from gonorrhea to anal dilatation plus bruises, or the children had made disclosures. In one case, the father had complained to Mr Bell, after he'd been pleading his innocence to the Rev Wright and the Parents Against Injustice group, which gave support to the Cleveland parents' group. Unknown to Mr Bell the man had seven convictions for sexual assaults on children. He had been interviewed on 13 June by a policewoman who, despite his denials, believed 'there is no doubt he is responsible for this assault'. But by then the police were not prosecuting sexual abuse cases, and the officer wrote in her contemporaneous notes: 'With the present policy I was unable to charge him with the offence.' A 'substantial proportion' of the cases Stuart Bell had adopted were, subsequently, confirmed as sexual abuse.

Stuart Bell's book on the Cleveland crisis, *When Salem Came to the Boro*, was published immediately after the Butler-Sloss inquiry team published its report in July 1988. The book claims to tell 'The True Story of the Cleveland Crisis' but doesn't so much tell the truth as throw down the gauntlet. In Bell's book, the medieval witches become not today's vilified paediatricians and social workers, but innocent parents damned by a new inquisition whose quest for the 'Devil's Mark' on the doomed women's bodies found its echo in the doctors' search for physical signs.

Salem's modern equivalent was the wanton purges of parents and wayward testimonies of children. The boro fathers' only defence, according to Bell, was 'a coalition of men of the cloth, Members of Parliament, the legal profession, the media and the police'. An invincible alliance – but to protect whom? A couple of Bell's classic case studies are paradigms of both his method and his message.

One case (see also p. 138) arose when a headmaster of a special school for disturbed children called in the father of an 11-year-old boy to tell him that the boy, along with several others in the school, had been sexually abused. When the boy's four-year-old sister was sent for a medical examination at Middlesbrough General, she too showed signs of sexual abuse. Bell tells us that the boy said he'd pushed pens up the girl.

But what Bell does not report is that both children said that they had been sexually abused by their father, and the girl said she had been abused by her brother, too. The father made an eight-page statement to the police after being arrested, apparently on the strength of previous sexual offences brought to the attention of the police by the children's social worker. He was not charged and there were no criminal proceedings. Nor does Bell tell us how the father tape-recorded his son's retraction of the allegations during a supervised access visit. Second opinions were sought and the medical signs were confirmed.

Mr Bell was right: there was no prosecution. But we might wonder why. Mr Justice Sheldon might have wondered why, too, during wardship proceedings involving these two children in January 1988, when the calumny against the anal dilatation diagnosis had calmed down. The shocked judge heard not only medical evidence but reports of severe emotional damage – and then banished the father from any further access to the children. Why doesn't Stuart Bell tell us that?

The same judge was to make an equally dramatic adjudication the following April which cast doubt on the role of Dr Myles Clarke, a police surgeon and one of the expert witnesses who gave evidence for dissenting parents during the Cleveland controversy. The judge concluded that, 'Dr Clarke seemed to me to be most reluctant to agree that Dr Higgs' diagnosis could be correct.' He added that, 'In the event I found his evidence unconvincing, particularly when contrasted with the clear, direct and unemotional manner in which she [Dr Higgs] had explained her conclusions. He gave me the impression that he was still fighting a battle that had been joined in regard to other facts in other fields . . . Nor was I left in any doubt that Dr Higgs' findings and conclusions were to be preferred.'

This case was a salient moment in the controversy, and as one legal expert commented, 'This was the same Dr Higgs who gave evidence in other cases, but what has been happening is that the credibility gap has been closed by a senior High Court judge in the calm light of day.'

Stuart Bell's book never acknowledges that once the dust began to settle, and once social workers and paediatricians emerged from the exhaustion of the crisis, their credibility began to be restored. But that's because he only ever tells one side of his stories.

Take the case of the man who tragically hanged himself in prison awaiting trial on allegations of abusing his daughters. They, too, had named their father, who they also loved, after signs of sexual abuse were found on their bodies. Their mother (see p. 182) had seen the much-maligned sign of anal dilatation and was amazed. And she believed her children when they described abuse by their father. Stuart Bell records how the dead man's family believed in his innocence, but his former wife is not consulted in his chronicle. Why not?

The whole book is like that. We're told the pitiable story of the man abandoned by his wife, who believed the diagnosis. What are we supposed to infer: that she's a bitch?

We're told in his book of children taken to outpatients with sore feet or something or other and then being whipped into hospital on a whimsical sexual abuse diagnosis, but what we're not told is that the children were medically examined by Dr Higgs and Dr Wyatt for possible sexual abuse because somebody somewhere was already worried about them. Nowhere does he qualify his claims with the benefit of hindsight after the challenges he faced during the judicial inquiry. It's as if the inquiry and its report had never happened.

Mr Bell was suspected by some of his constituents of opportunism in his handling of the crisis. Sitting one day in a Middlesbrough café, three women sat at my table and echoed a notion often heard in Middlesbrough at that time. What did they think of his campaign? 'Children don't have votes,' said one of them. Careerism was confirmed by another North-East MP, Frank Cook, who told the inquiry that Bell had said to him, in reference to Cook's popular anti-nuclear campaign in a neighbouring constituency, 'You had your Nirex, this is mine.'

Stuart Bell's campaign, however, revealed Labourism's confusions and conservatism about sexual politics. Early in June, Cleveland's social services committee was briefed about the sexual abuse volcano by Mike Bishop. But it became clear at the full committee's meeting on 24 June that many of the elected members still did not grasp what was going on. They remained more or less silent for the rest of the year, whilst all the major agencies responsible for child protection were stumbling around in a new era in the politics of child protection and of the family. It was a historic moment – nothing less than a fundamental challenge to the familial politics of Thatcherism, which sought to restore the absolute autonomy and authority of the patriarchal family. The party for the family was the party for fathers. But neither the county council's Labour group nor the region's Labour Party organised a single discussion amongst themselves or in local society about what the hell it all meant.

The councillors' political passivity and the party's self-obsession fatally excluded them from the public debate. And since the boundaries of that debate were defined by the *professional procedures* of child protection rather than the *politics* of child sexual abuse, those committed to challenging abuse were left without any independent room for manoeuvre, and were coralled into the county council's camp. As usual in the Labour Party's gothic moments, the political issue was engaged not in and for itself but as part of an inner-party struggle. The effect was a vacuum in Cleveland's civil society – into which stepped Stuart Bell, the Rev Wright, South Tees Community Health Council, local lawyers and the media, all of them co-ordinating the fathers' revolt against the community's elected council. Theirs was a powerful fraternity which carried the imprimateur of potent institutions supposed to serve the community: none of them, however, had organised actively against men's sexual abuse of children.

What was really a fathers' movement became represented as a campaign for the family, to which the support of mothers gave vital legitimacy. There appeared to be only two formations: the state, embodied in the county council and social workers, and the people, represented by the council's critics, whose space was civil society and whose language was common sense.

Sue Richardson – the men's target

In the aftermath of the crisis, social services, even more than the doctors or the hospital, were represented as the jackbooted stormtroopers busting up families, and at the centre of that image was Sue Richardson. We never learned who she was, where she lived, what pleased her or what animated her. She was a woman without a context, seen only when she was tense, urgent, striding along the street, flanked by lawyers on her way to the Town Hall. That was partly a function of a media commitment, whether conscious or not, to represent the women at the heart of the controversy as caricatures of the modern working woman, women outside the relationships by which women have traditionally been defined. It was also a self-conscious strategy adopted by the women at the heart of the controversy. 'As a woman you want to be accepted in your own right, so you play down your personal life because you don't want to be judged on it, as women usually are. We don't expect men to be contextualised, but we do expect that of woman. I take it as an insult, because it was usually done offensively, we *are* our functions, our roles,' said Sue Richardson.

We don't expect to know whether professional men have children, perhaps because it doesn't make any difference – they don't take care of them anyway, someone else does. But that's important: the fact that many male professionals have so little responsibility for the care of their children perhaps means that they wouldn't recognise a shut bum from a dilating anus. It is worth saying that men's irresponsible fatherhood is material to our social world and might have been salient to Cleveland's crisis. Likewise, the three most prominent women in the Cleveland controversy, Drs Jane Wynne, Marietta Higgs and Sue Richardson, are all mothers. The fact that Sue Richardson was primarily responsible for her teenage children tells us something about her which was denied in the windy snaps which appeared in the press during the inquiry. So, too, that she casually collected art-deco crockery, listened to Mozart as well as Joan Armatrading, and had on her shelves feminist thrillers, books on 'yoga for the over-40s' and 'lazy gardening'. She had helped start Middlesbrough's first women's group when Women's Liberation embraced Britain in 1970 and had a long-time connection with socialist-feminism along the North-East coast.

As a representative of the state, Sue Richardson

appeared not only to be attacking the rights of fathers, but of mothers, not least because the key word in the controversy became 'parents'. And in the name of children, whose rights were always ambiguous – did they have the right to stay at home or leave home? Could they ever determine the outcome of arrangements made on their behalf? – parents in general appeared to be the problem. There was no sense during the controversy, or in the representations of the major female characters, that mothers were felt to be different from fathers, that the state not only required mothers to protect their children, but that the state would support them in their efforts.

Instead, the state – personified ironically by a woman like Sue Richardson – which had historically given power to fathers, now appeared 'to take the role of patriarch itself'.[3] Suzanne Franzway's study of the role of feminism in the state when confronting sexual abuse in New South Wales, Australia, suggests that ironically, women have demanded state intervention to protect women and children from men. And yet, the state can appear to 'take the patriarchal right to make decisions about the child and relates to the mother through the child. As the state determines the rights as well as the needs of the child, the mother's parental rights are eroded.'[4] That became Sue Richardson's one source of regret – that no one empowered mothers during Cleveland's crisis.

The mothers – on their own

The redoubts of civil society represented in the fathers' coalition gave disbelief its moral mandate. There was nothing to match the successful campaign only a couple of years earlier to defend Wendy Savage, a consultant obstetrician at the London Hospital in the heart of the impoverished East End, who was harassed by male colleagues affronted by her campaign to give birth back to parents. The parents who mobilised for Wendy Savage when the hospital tried to dump her, and throughout the subsequent public inquiry, were defending an experience of parenthood of which they could be proud and pleased – a birth in which they had been participants rather than objects slotted into an induction schedule. Where she brought pleasure and power back into the moment of birth, the Cleveland case appeared to bring only pain. This perhaps helps explain why in Cleveland parents themselves didn't organise in support of the paediatricians or social services.

For mothers, particularly, there were few arms reaching out to hold them while they did what mothers always do: cope. For some mothers the pain of the discovery simply dramatised their isolation. They just wanted to recover themselves: to heal, not to organise. For what some of them had been faced with was the shocking realisation that the men they were or had been married to, whom they lived with and often loved, may have been abusing their children. Some of them may have suspected as much for a long time – have seen the signs and harboured fears – but for many the need *not* to believe was probably paramount. For to believe meant confronting the humiliating knowledge that the child had been both abused and, perhaps, sexually preferred. It also meant confronting their own vulnerability in the face of society's demand that they, as mothers, must protect – alone, if needs be.

For some mothers, solace was found among others at the Children's Resource Centre, where two counselling groups were organised to see mothers through the worst. 'What we saw was that there was no organised support for families,' said Debbie Glassbrook. 'It was non-existent apart from what Rev Wright organised. But a lot of mothers were left to care for abused children alone when they'd gone into shock themselves, because it had been done by someone they'd married or lived with and loved. There was the shock of the allegation itself – that they hadn't known. There was the embarrassment because they were thinking they'd been foolish for not spotting what was going on. Then there were the memories of their own sexuality – some had been abused in their own childhood. So there was the problem of how to cope with the children when they had their own feelings to cope with.

'These women were in trauma because they had accepted the diagnosis. Now they were on their own because of what had happened. The pain of what they were left with was enormous.'

Apart from the children's centre, nothing was organised in the community for women, or by women; no women's organisation joined the fray to endorse the fathers' revolt. There were more than a few households in Cleveland which always had arguments after child abuse appeared on the news, with husbands shouting at the pictures of Dr Higgs flashing across their screens and wives saying they bet the woman was right. But no women's organisation was able to take hold of the public debate and transform it.

Within Cleveland's civil society, then, the men made the running. Perhaps the debate was so focused on the professionals that any political intervention by women would have seemed like a defence of the state and the powers-that-be. The political culture had not encouraged organisations belonging to the community to take on child abuse apart from the networks built by women to support battered wives and the survivors of sexual assault, which were wholly marginalised during the great debate. Nor had adequate links been created between the local state and civil society to safeguard the discovery of sexual abuse. 'The gap between the professionals and self-help groups was crucial,' said Sue Richardson.

The irony was that only social services, not civil society, took responsibility for intervening to protect children, and yet it appeared to do so in a way that attacked the community. At the same time, social services was the only agency involved which was within the direct political control of the community – it was, after all, administered and employed formally at least by the community's elected representatives. It was they who remained speechless throughout.

The men's movement was classically populist – it articulated a revolt against professional power and yet it did so in the name not of the powerless – the children – but of the traditional authority of fathers within the family.

The Social Services Inspectorate – does the government get the answers it wants?

Throughout the crisis the Social Services Inspectorate, an arm of the government charged with investigating and monitoring social work departments, had scrutinised the efforts to respond to the evidence and the calumny it was causing. The SSI reassured the county that they were not alone – there were professional conflicts and proliferating caseloads in many parts of the country.

The crisis was being monitored, therefore, at the highest level. Social workers' dilemmas were known to their own managers, who, in turn, consulted their own directorate and the independent inspectorate.

The same was not true of the police. Although Mike Bishop and other senior managers were aware that their staff felt intimidated by police officers, and although the police resisted the new culture of child protection, the Chief Constable was ignorant of the volcano erupting in his force. On 22 May the Director and the Chief Constable found themselves face to face at a social event and Mike Bishop alerted him to the conflict. It was the first the Chief Constable had heard of it. So ignorant were senior police managers of their sister services that a senior police officer thought Dr Higgs was a social services employee.

By the end of May the police had pulled out of the multi-disciplinary process. This was war. War was formally declared on 29 June, when the police went public.

But at no point in this affray did the SSI dissent from the department and Bishop's approach. The SSI was still supporting the department's general approach when Stuart Bell accused social services of 'conspiring and colluding' and also of empire-building – an allegation that astonished staff servicing a county with the highest unemployment in England on a budget below the national average.

The SSI was aware of Bell's charges, investigated them and, after a searching visit during the early summer by four inspectors, rejected them. The SSI's *Report on Child Sexual Abuse in Cleveland* was published early in July and it was unequivocal: 'No evidence of a conspiracy or collusion against parents or any attempt to manipulate the local authority to gain more resources has been uncovered.' So Stuart Bell was wrong.

Apart from confronting the critics, the SSI report usefully tabulated the cases, the sources of referral, the number of medical diagnoses and the corroborative evidence. This dispensed with notions of routine screening and rumours of respectable families being raided at the whim of witchdoctors.

Crucially, the SSI showed that in about half of the cases sexual abuse had been exposed by the children themselves, or professional worries had been confirmed. The other cases had been referred by the hospital. These children had, of course, already been referred to the hospital because of other people's professional concerns. This fact confounded the tendency to locate the evidence in doctors' fantasies rather than the children themselves – scripted on their bodies and in the spoken word. The SSI report suggested that the inter-agency difficulties, the use of the courts and the way parents were being informed – the paediatricians believed in sharing their concerns with parents immediately – be reviewed. It also aired social workers' concern that as long ago as 1985–6, when, for the first time, the government had required local authorities to specify sexual abuse in their guidelines, the police and the police surgeons had mutinied, and so the new arrangements were 'never implemented'. No minister was prompted to call the police to account. Nor was the government mindful that the agency most dismissive of the evidence was also most alienated from its own procedures and from modern child protection practice.

This was a crucial intervention because the public debate had been driven so far by the police and by Stuart Bell. Bell's tactics in June and July had implied that the government did not know what was going on. But the SSI is an arm of government, it had been consulted throughout the crisis by the Cleveland Social Services Department, and anyway the government itself had dispatched those four inspectors. So the local authority had ensured that the highest levels of government were alerted to events in the county.

The SSI report acknowledged that the department had 'kept the SSI fully involved' and that its overall strategy had been 'professionally positive and responsive to government policy'. But the extent to which the SSI was heeded by the government can be discerned from the sequence of events that summer.

Stuart Bell told his story to the Health Minister at the end of June, *before* publication of the SSI report on 2 July. On 6 July he presented a dossier of protests by parents, supported by the police. On 9 July the government announced a judicial inquiry into the management of the crisis – the very issue that had already been investigated by its own inspectors. Bell had triumphed. His claim that Cleveland County Council had launched a 'fundamental attack on family life' no doubt resonated with a government pledged to the restoration of traditional family values.

The government had made a choice between the MP and the SSI. There was an obvious inference: the SSI – the government's professional adjudicators – had not given ministers what they wanted. Populist politics, rather than professional judgement, was clearly driving the Department of Health.

Family sagas

A respectable father

During 1987 and 1988 several parents whose children were believed to have been abused went public with their protest. These parents were professional people. Their class and status were mobilised with spectacular success to refute the charge that their children, whose bodies showed dramatic signs of chronic buggery, had been abused. They were the jewel in the crown of the Parents Support Group. Their reputation as respectable people was confidently cited as *evidence* of the impossibility of abuse.

One couple's youngest son, still a toddler, had been referred by the family doctor to Dr Higgs because of a persistent problem with his bottom, which had come to dominate the domestic life of the family. The family doctor did not accept the possibility of abuse – the family were his friends, he said.

Dr Higgs saw the child and suspected sexual abuse. She asked that the two other children be brought in for an examination and found what she believed were signs consistent with anal abuse. The parents were informed. The mother became fearfully upset. The father apparently was not alarmed; he said he believed Dr Higgs was simply wrong. When Dr Higgs told them that she would have to call the police the mother was shocked and the father said he thought it was ridiculous.

Why didn't the father wonder, as a parent might, what the diagnosis meant and ask himself who might be responsible, or how his children were feeling? Why didn't he feel – as many parents do in the same situation, rightly or wrongly – guilty, not only because he might be suspected as the perpetrator but because he had failed to protect his children?

The father then feared that he would be seen as the abuser, although he later said he had never thought of himself as the prime suspect. The police interrogated the children, telling them that they *knew* something had happened, and then accused them of lying and wasting police time. The father, too, was subjected to many hours of interrogation. He insisted that he had not abused his children and could not conceive of anyone else abusing them either. Only when the police suggested that one of the children might be responsible did he concede that yes, perhaps that was the explanation. Dr Higgs and Sue Richardson were later to protest at the police interrogation of this boy.

Undoubtedly the police were influenced by the children's response to Dr Higgs' description of their medical problem – it had always been her practice to explain symptoms to parents and to patients. The police, therefore, were aware of the children's assent when told that it seemed as though someone had put something up them. Both the boy and the girl agreed that an adult at home had been doing this – but they wouldn't say who. The girl added that her brother pushed his fingers up her. Although the police interrogation appeared to be hard and horrible, it had been prompted by clues from the children themselves.

Several independent opinions were mobilised. The emerging consensus among the doctors was that there was compelling physical evidence of abuse – not just one child but all three children in this family had severe anal signs, according to all the medical experts except Dr Raine Roberts, who was finally enlisted on behalf of the parents four months after the original diagnosis.

After some initial doubts, when the mother contemplated the possibility that the father had abused the children, the parents were united in their dissent from the diagnosis. And so, in the absence of any alternative medical explanation, the older children were taken into care and the youngest was looked after by a close friend.

In April the youngest child, whose bowel problems were severe, was seen by a prestigious Newcastle paediatrician, Dr Hans Steiner, a member of the Independent Panel, who was well known for his cautious, not to say rather conservative, approach to child abuse. His first report, produced in April for the civil court, commented that the appearance of the child's anus could be compatible with constipation and bowel problems, but added that 'this does not exclude the possibility of sexual abuse'. He stressed the need for corroborative evidence.

Corroborative evidence apparently arrived when he saw the photographs of this little boy's older brother and sister – their bodies showed signs consistent with chronic buggery. Dr Steiner was chastened. Having offered an ambiguous – 'it could be, but it might not be' – assessment, he was stirred by these forensic photographs. According to the mother, the parents had believed that this assessment meant they were in the clear. 'We thought it was all over.'[5] But when he saw those pictures Dr Steiner became solemn and told the parents that he could not challenge Dr Higgs' diagnosis. This was a devastating blow. It was one thing for the diagnosis to be dismissed by Dr Roberts – she had always done so and had argued against the existence of any anal signs – but quite another for the middle-of-the-road Dr Steiner, upon whom the father depended, to be confirming the diagnosis.

The regular case conferences, which had been held since the children were seen in hospital in the middle of March, continued to hear that the older children, who were quiet and distressed, were making oblique and qualified allusions to what might have been happening at home. Certainly, at that time their ambivalence was susceptible to many interpretations, and their comments would not have supported a criminal case. But the case conferences heard sufficiently worrying reports from social workers, paediatricians, psychologists and foster carers to support their worst fears about the meaning of the strong medical signs. They heard that the elder boy had talked about his father and written many pages with the word 'Dad' scrawled all over them; that the mother had seen a video in which he said he wanted the adults responsible, by which he meant 'Mum and Dad', to 'come forward'; and that the daughter had said that her father had abused her. By the autumn, however – when the children were aware of the Parents Support Group's campaign, which was well publicised in the local media – the children retracted their comments implicating their father.

During the spring and summer the professionals had confronted the father with the suspicions that he was the perpetrator. In front of his tearful children he resolutely denied the allegations. The professionals also shared the children's comments with the mother, whose distress produced pity and alarm in the children. She said she was unmoved by her children's hesitant remarks. She said she just didn't see anything in them, unlike the practitioners, who were persuaded that these children were silenced and frightened. But the mother insisted to the professionals that nothing short of a categorical statement would persuade her.

In a detailed interview that the parents gave to the *Sunday Times*, published in May 1988, they referred neither to the concentrated efforts by the professionals to engage the mother nor to the children's comments passed on to her.

The parents had been given to understand that the symptoms were so serious that unless a perpetrator was identified – and given the children's allusions to their father, he was clearly a prime suspect – the children would have to remain the subjects of a Place of Safety Order. In May the father's access to the children was stopped and the High Court appointed a guardian *ad litem*, an independent professional expected to work with the children's interests uppermost and accountable only to the court. In October the children returned home. The police had by then broken away from the inter-disciplinary team and the case was soon to be heard by the High Court. Two weeks before the hearing the County Council pulled out, having heard from a QC that in the current atmosphere they would be unlikely to win and might incur hefty costs.

When the family appeared before Mr Justice Eastham two weeks later he took the children aside and told them that they had not been abused and that their father was not an abuser.

All parties involved, including the judge presumably, had seen the report by the High Court's own appointee, the guardian *ad litem*. Although strictly confidential, it was fairly widely distributed: there were a lot of protagonists pitching in this case – parents, children, police, social services, and solicitors representing all of them. It was not impossible to get hold of a copy from one or other of them. But although the case received considerable press attention, the guardian's report was never leaked. When the judge told the children that they had not been abused had he read the paragraph in which the guardian *ad litem* concluded that there was every possibility that the children had been abused?

After the children returned home an investigation was launched into the alleged abuse of children by a worker at the special school where the father was a teacher. The case never came to court, but the children received criminal injuries compensation. The father was also the subject of a separate allegation, which was never investigated.

'I did the best I could'

Jean Strong is a stoical woman who was living alone with her three young daughters in one of the many treeless terraced streets surrounding the centre of Middlesbrough. She kept a diary in a spiral notebook after May 1987. *Private, Keep Out* it said on the front. On the back she had drawn a heart and inside the heart she had written *RIP*. Her former husband hanged himself in prison where he was being detained for alleged sexual abuse of his daughters.

'I don't agree with people trying to get rid of Dr Higgs, because other people won't speak out, and the same thing will happen to other people as happened to my daughters.

'It began when my two-year-old, Beverley, had a convulsion. She'd never had anything like that before, but a fortnight earlier she was bleeding from her backside. The health clinic said she might be constipated. It just didn't seem like it, but I changed her diet anyway to bran fibre and fresh oranges. The very next day she was very loose, so I eased up. When her bowels opened she bled, but only at odd times. So one Friday I phoned the doctor who just said it was constipation, change her diet. I said, "I've done that and I've been to the clinic."

'She bled again on the Monday so I decided to take her to the doctor the next day. But she had the convulsion when I took my two older daughters to school. We got an ambulance to casualty and I mentioned the bleeding, so they admitted her.

'Later in the week the doctor came to examine her and asked if they could take a photograph of her backside to help find out what was wrong, and I said yes. The nurse said Dr Higgs might want a word with me about the other two. When I asked her what it was about, she said, "I don't really know, and I'm not really supposed to say anything in case I'm wrong."

'I don't know how to say it but I had an idea it wasn't all right between the children and their father – he and I were separated – because the middle one didn't want to go away with him. This triggered something in my mind. I kept thinking, "Is it . . .?"

'He'd turned up out of the blue to take the older two girls for a week. The middle one, Carla, didn't want to go.

I said, "He loves you and wants you with him – it's like a holiday." But he came back with her in tears. His girlfriend thought she had mumps because her neck was all swollen. Carla was very tense and it was three days before she relaxed. She wouldn't tell me why, but she didn't want to go back to her father.

'The weekend before the convulsions, he'd come and collected Alison but Carla broke her heart, she didn't want to go. I don't like to say it, but I did worry whether anything had happened to her in *that way*. When they all came home he took the little one up to bed. I said, "Now you go to bed with Daddy." She flew across the room and stood there, frozen, and then had that look as if to say, "Well, I'd better – there's no other way." I only thought about that afterwards.

'Anyway in the week the little one, Beverley, was in hospital, I mentioned the photographs at the hospital to my husband and asked if he was coming as well to see what it was. We all went. Dr Higgs asked all the normal questions about the health of the children. My husband wanted to know if it was hereditary, because he'd since had a son. She said she'd just examine the children. She was polite, she'd introduced herself and took all the particulars, and then said to Alison she was going to examine her. She did ears, nose, throat, all the checks, and then asked her to turn over. She didn't poke or prod, she just looked, calmly and gently, and said, "That's all right", and then did the same with Carla.

'But I could tell there was something wrong because when she parted the cheeks of her bottom, I saw it open. I was totally agog. I thought there was something wrong because they're usually tight closed. It totally astounded me. I was wondering what this was all about. Dr Higgs was just telling Carla what she was doing: she was good with her, not forceful. She told her how to position her legs, said, "Put your knees up" and put her feet together, and Carla seemed to do it automatically – I thought this wasn't right.

'Dr Higgs said, "I'm sorry, but all three of your children have been sexually abused."

'I'm a funny person, I don't react, I don't express feelings. I was just frozen. I was very grateful to her, and thanked her for what she'd explained, because it meant they didn't need to go through so much again. I said, "Do you know something, I'd half expected you to say that." She said, "Why? Who do you think it could be?" I said they were with me 24 hours a day and the only time they were out of my sight was when they went to their father's. In other words, I didn't know who touched them when they went there. I didn't mean it was him. She talked with me for a while and said she had to tell my husband. I said, "Be careful, take somebody with you because he might not take it very well."

'I was crying my eyes out, totally devastated, when he came out of the cubicle. He stood at the doorway of the cubicle, calm as you like. He said, "I've been told to stay away from my kids, you said it was me." I said, "I didn't but you tell me who it is." He was too calm. Normally he'd explode and want to get hold of whoever had done it.

'They let me alone for a while, and as we were arguing Dr Higgs came for her notes and she whispered to me, "Are you all right?" I nodded and after he went, a nurse offered me some tea. They were marvellous.

'The police came, that's the next thing I remember – two detectives, a man and a woman. We went into another room and talked about it. They wanted to know about his sexual behaviour, and I told them there was lots that was unusual about it. They talked to Dr Higgs and mentioned something about an examination and they'd brought a police surgeon. The next day, I put my arms round Beverley and said, "You're all right, you're safe with mammy," and then she put her arms tight round my neck. Alison seemed upset and said, "They poked my bum," and I said, "Has anybody else poked your bum?" and she said, "yes", but I wasn't in any fit state to go any further. They'd taken a swab, you see. Carla seemed to be defensive. All we got out of Alison was that she and Carla had a secret.

'My social worker took me out for my dinner, because I'd taken a lot and needed time for myself. Alison told the police what happened and who had done it. Carla told them what had happened, but not who'd done it. The woman detective said she'd have to take it to a superior to see if they could arrest him.

'They took him into custody. They needed a holding charge. They wanted to get him for sodomy, so they gave me an examination. They said they couldn't charge him for the children, they needed some more time to see if he would admit it. He wouldn't.

'The girls loved their father and get very upset now thinking about it. They don't say anything. Carla occasionally says a little bit if something comes up. I try to make them aware that what happened doesn't have to happen. When I told Carla it had happened to Beverley, she said, "How could it, she never went there?" which shows she feels safe here.

'On 29 July he died. People say to me, "Are you sure he did it?" and I say, "Well, the kids said he did."

'I'm pushing for the girls to see somebody. I went to a group run at the Children's Resource Centre for mothers of abused children. It only lasted for a short time – eight weeks in the autumn – but I found it very good. A few of us found it beneficial because we could compare our children's behaviour, so you knew what was part of getting over the abuse. A friend had her children at the resource centre, too and when my children met them I outlined that mine had been abused as well. And they told each other – that was good, it seemed to put Carla's mind at rest. And my friend was pleased that her daughter could talk about it. I think they need to talk it out.

'I've got a lot of friends who are very good. But I feel trapped a heck of a lot. I'm here with three children. I've no outlet, I don't go out. There's nothing anybody can do about it. The police told Carla she was a very good girl and promised her a trip round the police station, but since her father died they didn't bother. They came round to bring back the birth certificates and I told them she was still waiting for the visit. I feel I'm pestering people if I push it. A lot of times, when you talk about it all, you feel you are pestering, going on about it too much. I haven't got it straight in my mind. I didn't *want* to believe it and I still find it hard. I'd have felt happier if it could have gone to court and the jury could have decided rather than me having to think about it.

'I never got to hate him for it, I pitied him. I wish I could have hated him. I hated what he did, and for deceiving the children by making them think this was what happened to everybody. That destroyed their trust. A friend of mine says that if her husband did anything like that she'd kill him, but when it happens you don't. Actually, you blame yourself. I've done that, thinking I made him do this, but I can't figure out what it was I did.

'I told the children their father had gone into hospital and then that he had died. I was too upset to wait and so I told them right away. I did the best I could.'

Middlesbrough's *Evening Gazette* at this time was campaigning against Dr Higgs and regularly ran pieces on its front page accompanied by its logo saying, 'Give Us Back Our Children'. It announced the death on its front page. 'Child Care Dad's Jail Cell Suicide', and reported the father and sisters of the dead man saying not only that they believed he was innocent, but that 'the children had been returned to their mother after doctors decided that they had not been abused'. There was no comment from the doctors or the children's mother. A week later a correction appeared at the bottom of the letters page from the mother reporting that the Regional Health Authority's second opinion panel had confirmed that the physical assessment of the children was 'consistent with sexual abuse. The probabilities are extremely high.'

A man of conviction

During the height of the crisis, a man with previous convictions for sex offences against children was brought in by Cleveland police for questioning about suspected sexual abuse of his own children. They interrogated the man, Sidney (not his real name; the names of all family members have been changed), a week after medical examinations yielded worrying anal and vaginal signs on his daughters.

'I'd been done 16 years before for under-age sex,' he said, 'so I knew there was no getting away from it, I was going to be blamed. I knew two people who'd already had their children taken away because of the same thing, so I knew they'd take mine away.'

However, his offences were hardly 'under-age sex', a term implying the victim's consent. He had been convicted for offences against a six-year-old girl, and his admitted offences against about 15 other girls were 'taken into consideration'. He was also convicted of the attempted rape of a teenager.

But Sidney's expectations were to be curiously confounded. During his interrogation, he confessed. Suddenly police hostility changed to camaraderie. They didn't take his confession seriously, they said, because they didn't take the signs seriously. Indeed, it was as if they wanted not to find him guilty, but to find Dr Higgs guilty.

Sidney Actually, they were very nice. Well, for the first day they were trying to tell me I'd done it, which was normal. They said where and how the children had been abused – by two fingers. For the first five hours it was up to me to prove I hadn't. It was, 'How often are you at home with the children? How often do you touch them? Do you mess about with them?' He wasn't so much asking me, as telling me. He told me, 'I cuddle my children in places I shouldn't, you know, do you do that?' The implication was, 'Obviously you do, because your children have been abused.' So you could say it was laughable, because he was telling me he did things to his daughter, that there was nothing to be ashamed of.

But initially, it was force. He'd say, 'Don't get stroppy with me, son.' He even called me a dirty little bastard. I said, 'I'm not.'

To be quite honest, I cannot explain how I felt, I can't tell you how they treated me because I wasn't there in my mind. I was there but I wasn't. He was grabbing me by the tie and I was just looking into space. Oh, it was heavy interrogation for hours. He asked about anyone who was in close contact with the children. I had to convince them it wasn't Lorna, that it wasn't Brian, my partner. If the children had shown any signs of fear in relation to them, I'd have noticed it.

That way of interrogating you makes you give in, I even told them I'd done it to get out of the police station – it's the most horrible place in the world. You've got people, six or seven other police station officers, poking their heads round the door, just to have a look at you, and then walking out with a look of disgust. It had all been planned to humiliate me. To be quite honest, I thought they were going to pin it on me, so it didn't make any difference.

But then the detective's attitude changed. He left me alone for a few hours. To be honest, he didn't want to know. He tried his best to get it out of me but after the first five hours his attitude completely changed. He came back and he was a totally different man, he had a smile on his face, he asked if I wanted a cup of tea. I said, 'What's this, the nice guy treatment?'

He said, 'No, to be quite honest, I don't believe your children have been abused.' I said, 'How do you make that out?' He said, 'Well, to be quite honest, you're not the first one who's been brought in and swears they're innocent.' It was him who told us about the outbreak of sexual abuse. And that's when he asked if I'd go for a second opinion. I said, 'What the hell will that do?' He said, 'We have no faith in Marietta Higgs.' So, that was it. I was on top of the world.

The saga had begun when Sidney set up home with Lorna: both had children from previous relationships. Sidney's wife had left him and their two daughters, who were then five and four years old. She hated and feared him. A troubled woman, she got out and early in 1987 hoped to get her children out. She failed. Despite sharing her anxieties with the court, her husband was given custody of the children.

By then Sidney had met Lorna at a local authority Family Centre where he was receiving parenting support and working as a voluntary driver, and she was helping teach dressmaking and toymaking skills. She had a horrendous history, a narrative that belonged to the pre-history of contemporary child politics. She had been put in care herself when she was only six years old. Typically, when she told staff at the children's home that she had been sexually abused by a housefather, she was not believed. When another young woman made allegations against the same man, corroborated by other girls, there was belief – but also blame.

In the early 1980s several children in the neighbourhood had been abused by a local man, a neighbour. A little later, Lorna had a severe breakdown and her own children were received into care. When Sidney and Lorna began living together, enjoying the support of the Family Centre, she started looking after his two deeply troubled daughters and wanted her children to join them in the newly configured family. Her eldest daughter, Lisa, returned home in the spring, her second daughter, Sarah, visited regularly, although she remained in care, and her third child joined the new family.

Sidney's daughters were still the subject of Supervision Orders – a device often used in those days to keep an eye on children – and an application was made to Teesside Magistrates in January 1987 to lift those Supervision Orders. But the application was postponed pending the custody case between Sidney and his former wife and the production of a Probation report.

In May social workers were given the stunning news that this man had a history of serious sex offences against children. Staff who had been keen to support the new family suddenly had to stop and think. Sue Richardson suggested a case conference and a medical examination of Sidney's two daughters and Lorna's girls.

They went to Middlesbrough General on June 9.

Sidney's children had been admitted to hospital before, but Lorna's children were healthy.

Sidney I didn't know at the time what sort of examination it was going to be, I thought it was just an up and down medical, I didn't know it was going to be an internal medical. Lorna stayed with the children when they were seen by Dr Higgs that afternoon after a long wait.

Lorna There was nothing wrong with any of them. She examined their ears etc., and then their bottoms, back and front. On the two little girls they used a glass rod in the vagina. Dr Higgs didn't explain why she was doing that. I held their hands and I actually had my coat over their heads because they didn't want to look – they were bashful, you know what kids are like. When the last one went out, Dr Higgs said, 'I'm sorry, your children aren't going home tonight, they've been abused.' She told me what she'd seen: anal and vaginal abuse of the little one, who was five, vaginal abuse of the middle one, who was six, and anal abuse of the oldest, who was seven. She said one of them had a bad scar that had been there a long time, plus other scars and anal dilatation. The only thing that was there was Emily has a habit of coming downstairs on her backside – she's always done it – and she had little bruises, and they said the bruises were fingertip bruises where she'd been held and forced down. A social worker said they'd take them into care for a few days. They didn't ask me, they just told me.

So children referred for a medical examination because they were living with a convicted sex offender were found to have significant signs of abuse. Sidney's five-year-old daughter had bruises on her buttock and waist, consistent, it was said, with having been held down, and hymenal tears and other irregularities. Her younger sister also had hymenal tears, together with anal signs, including anal dilatation. Lorna's eight-year-old daughter had anal and vaginal scars and fissures; she had been abused by a neighbour three years earlier. And Lorna's six-year-old daughter, who was still in care but regularly visiting her mother, also showed some physical signs. These two children also had threadworms.

After Sydney's confession, the Cleveland police proposed getting a second opinion. No doubt their own police surgeon, Dr Irvine, would have supported their scepticism.

Sidney It was actually the detective who got us to get a second opinion. They were going to go for Dr Irvine, but I said I wanted somebody completely independent. I believed the police surgeon would collaborate with the police – I thought he'd say I'd done it. My solicitor suggested Dr Myles Clarke, because he was already handling other cases.

Dr Clarke, who gave many second opinions in the Cleveland controversy, saw the children and concluded that there were hymenal and anal irregularities but he assigned to these signs different *medical meanings* from those inferred by Dr Higgs.

Lorna When Dr Higgs told me she thought they'd been sexually abused, I started shouting, I kept saying 'It's history repeating itself, they couldn't do it last time, so they've done it this time.' You see, I was sexually abused when I was a kid in a children's home, and I was told I was a liar.

It just felt like they were saying, 'We'll have you again,

we'll put you through it all again.' I just went crazy and started screaming. I'd never told anybody about it, not even Sidney. I'd been abused by the housefather when I was about 11 or 12, and it turned out that a lot of the lasses had been abused at the time. One of the lasses who'd left came back on a visit, and he'd started on her again. She'd told somebody one day and they said she should report it. So that's how it came to a head. The police came and interviewed us, but then when we went to court there was the housefather sat in front of us and not one of us could open our mouths, because we knew we had to go back and live there. So we all clammed up. He got found not guilty, then he was given a nice fat pension and retired.

After that the man who used to collect the church collection started on the lasses from the home, and when we reported him they just said to us, 'You've lost one person his job, now do you want to lose someone else his job?' Every time we said anything about a man, they'd say it again, and they said, 'You lie about men.' They just got paranoid.

Nobody knew. And the files had been lost. They only turned up when a social worker from the Family Centre went searching for them, because she said we should go through them and find out exactly what happened. She was flabbergasted, because in those days they'd never sent a social worker to look after us. Everybody was told that I should never be left alone with a man because I might accuse him. So, I got blamed. That's when I started to not trust anybody.

It's taken me years to learn to cool down and not to blow up at things. It's taken me a long time becoming what I am. And my relationship with Sidney was very important because I felt it was the first time things were really working out.

When Dr Higgs said she thought my children had been abused, it felt to me, in that minute, that it was all happening again, that I was the one who was going to have to go through it.

When we were kids, the adults were believed and the kids weren't. Now it's the other way round. The parents aren't believed, and the children are, whether they tell the truth or not.'

Throughout the whole process, the custody dispute and the new suspicions of sexual abuse, Sidney's previous convictions – the most obvious indicator of a sexual interest in children – never seemed to influence the courts, the police or the police surgeon.

Sidney had lived with one vulnerable woman, and was now living with another, Lorna. Suspected sexual abuse uncovered the iceberg which had been floating around her own life. She had to deal not only with her own trauma but with the problem of the truth. When she was alerted to new suspicions she says her world crashed.

Lorna At that minute I believed it. I don't know that I even believed it so much as I was told it, and that's the way I believed it. You get so muddled up that you actually do believe it.

The social workers were saying did I ever know that Sidney was doing this, and you are in such a way with yourself, you are hearing so many things, so many times, you start to believe it.

Sidney Did you think I'd done it? You did, didn't you? She stopped sleeping with me. She believed I'd done it, which I don't blame her for. It's ruined our lives, this, I don't think we'll ever get over it.

Lorna I became doubtful and I decided he couldn't have

done it, because one of my kids said her father had done it, but he couldn't have. She'd said that my ex-husband had abused her – she told us how, and everything. Then the following week she told the social worker sorry, she was lying.'

But then Lorna began to have her doubts. She was under enormous pressure: from Sidney himself, despite his confession (now retracted), from the police and the Family Centre, and from the outside world and the media – during June and July the Middlesbrough MP had become a vocal and very visible protagonist in support of police disbelief in the diagnosis. Dissenting parents, too, were beginning to go public.

And then there was the response of the children. Although one of Sidney's daughters shared some worrying information with a foster carer, little was said. Lorna's eldest daughter, Lisa, said she had been sexually abused by her own father, Lorna's ex-husband – who was in prison at the time – but later retracted. In the chaos and confusion, Lisa remembers, she thought that since he was in prison nothing new and terrible would happen to him and he might get help.

Sidney I asked her [Lisa], in front of a social worker, if I'd ever touched her where I shouldn't. She said, 'Don't be stupid.' I thought I was doing the right thing by asking, but the social worker said later that I had no right to put a child in that predicament.
Lorna We know Lisa, and that's the kind of predicament she'd rather be in – she prefers straight questions and straight answers. That's what made us angry with the social workers, they didn't ask direct. I think she had a good inkling what was going on, because of the medical

and then all those people asking about whether somebody had touched her. I think she got the gist of what was going on.'

Either way, here was a little girl whose homecoming had been shaken by yet another crisis.

There was no investigation into the diverse signs, symptoms and suspicions of abuse. The children became the subject of wardship proceedings on 3 July. Sidney was arrested but released on police bail on 16 July; he was never charged with any offence. In November the children returned home to Sidney and Lorna, with the Supervision Orders still in place.

Lorna remembers that things then started to go very wrong. She says Sidney took resources from their joint business, he controlled her friendships and connections with the outside world – no sooner would she have arrived at a friend's home than he was on the telephone demanding to know when she was coming home – and he routinely humiliated her. Already lacking in self-esteem, she became more and more isolated and harassed.

He rehearsed his daughters in tantrums to be thrown at social workers – she remembers the girls throwing their breakfasts as the social worker came through the door. Whenever his daughters were due to visit their mother, he ranted his rageful denigration of 'that cow'. Lorna noticed, nevertheless, that they seemed to have an agreeable time with her. Their life with Sidney, then, was defined by chaos, conflict and control.

All that stopped six years later, when Lisa was 15 years old. He had encouraged her to go on the pill when she was about 13. He gave her drink. Sometimes she couldn't remember what happened next. He molested one of her friends – representing the relationship as an affair. But in May she told her mother that he had been sexually abusing her for about two years. Lorna instantly believed her and they left him. Social workers and the police believed her, too. The investigation revealed that her school work had slumped since the inception of the alleged abuse.

In 1995 her allegations of abuse brought Sidney to the criminal court in Teesside. Defence lawyers confronted both Lorna and Lisa with the events of 1987. Had Lisa not lied then? Had she not named a man who was in prison? 'Yes, but . . .' they tried to explain. The court was allowed to hear no more. He was acquitted.

It was as if the Cleveland stigma had come back, not to haunt Sidney but to save him; as if he had been given a certificate saying, 'Innocent'.

Courtroom dramas

During the summer the revolt against the diagnosis had a dramatic impact on the courts. The courts, in turn, stirred the public debate. In a couple of cases judges adjudicating in confidential civil proceedings took the rare step of making their findings public.

An audience of millions watching the Nine O'Clock News was left in no doubt that Cleveland's crisis had been caused by ignorant and arrogant zealots when Judge Hall's scornful judgment was aired on 18 August. No other ruling attracted the same attention.

The case concerned three children who had been referred to Dr Wyatt. All three were underweight and showed signs of neglect. The case was ignited by the bleeding vulva of one child. When she was examined by Dr Wyatt, he also noticed 'quite chronic' hymenal ruptures and signs of buggery. Dr Raine Roberts was brought in as a second opinion. She saw 'no abnormality' on this child and attributed suspicious signs on another child to 'rubbing' and 'threadworms', and bruising on the third child as 'rough play'.

'There is now a head-on conflict of opinion between Drs Wyatt and Roberts,' commented the judge, who preferred Dr Roberts' expertise and sent the children home.

Having a different view was represented as getting it wrong. And getting it wrong was news. Getting it right wasn't. Court judgments that vindicated the diagnosis never attracted the same attention.

Several months later, when the same protagonists appeared in the courts rehearsing the same arguments an experienced wardship judge, Mr Justice Sheldon, weighing professional judgements rather than reputations, drew different conclusions.

One case involved the two children of a convicted sex offender (see pp. 138–41), an 11-year-old boy and a four-year-old girl. When the boy was six, his father had pleaded guilty at Guisborough Magistrates Court to indecently assaulting children. The same year the boy was referred to psychologists for learning and behaviour difficulties, and he spent the next five years in special schools and hospitals as a psychiatric in-patient. No one made the connection between the father's conviction as a sex offender and the boy's troubles.

Lord Justice Butler-Sloss later told colleagues in the Medico-Legal Society in London in 1989 about this case. 'I particularly remember' this boy, she said, because although the majority of the Cleveland children did not speak, he was one of those who did, 'who for two years was telling the child psychiatrist about exactly how his father was committing serious anal abuse upon him. The child psychiatrist said that he was fantasising – and we were back to Freud.'

When he was 11, at a time when he was telling his psychiatrist that his father was buggering him, this boy was discovered by staff at his special school to be involved in sexual activities with another pupil. He also told staff that he had 'done things' to his little sister. The school did not refer him to the social services.

In June, however, the other pupil at the special school came to Dr Wyatt's attention. He saw signs of sexual abuse and asked to see other boys at the same school. The school would not agree to this – except in the case of the boy caught with the sex offender's son. When Dr Wyatt examined this boy and his little sister, he saw suspicious signs on both children. They were taken into care and instantly the boy began talking about what happened at home, how his father buggered him and made him abuse his sister, too. The little girl also described how her father had hurt her bottom and also buggered her brother and her mother. The judge remarked, presciently, that, despite the powerful evidence, the boy retracted his own statements against his father, even though throughout his life he had received from this man little more than 'criticism, denigration and abuse'.

In June, because of disagreements over the diagnosis, the children were seen by members of the regional health authority's second opinion panel. They were powerful and rather conservative but they felt that the evidence supported Dr Wyatt. The parents passed on all the records to third and fourth opinions, two police surgeons. The judge noted that they had already criticised Higgs and Wyatt and 'perhaps it came as no surprise' that they did so again. 'Each came to the conclusion that there was no medical evidence.' The judge came to a different conclusion.

This was an emblematic case: a learning-disabled child trying for two years to tell, while the psychoanalytic establishment re-interpreted his determined narrative. The child was, at last, taken seriously, by Dr Wyatt when he saw the stark signs written across his body. The boy later retracted his allegations against his adored, and abusive, father, only to repeat them, and only to have his story corroborated by his little sister. Yet the police surgeons would still have none of it.

Mr Justice Sheldon gave his judgment in another Cleveland case in April 1988. It concerned a girl referred to the hospital because of a chronic vaginal discharge. The offensive smell brought bullying and teasing at school. Her own GP noted vaginal abnormalities and referred her to Dr Higgs, who saw her in March and recorded other suspicious signs. At last the girl had someone to tell: a compelling case of sexual abuse emerged when she told social workers and psychologist Heather Bacon that she was being abused by her father. Though she occasionally retracted, she also repeated these allegations.

Altogether 19 people, including the parents, gave evidence to the judge. Their expert witness was Dr Myles Clarke who 'discounted entirely the significance attached by Dr Higgs to the dilatation of the hymen'. The judge found him unconvincing 'particularly when contrasted with the clear, direct and unemotional manner in which Dr Higgs had explained her conclusions. He gave me the impression that he was still fighting a battle that had been joined in regard to other facts in other fields.'

Mr Justice Sheldon vindicated the Cleveland professionals and these children were protected. But it was all too late to have any impact on the debate. Even before the Butler-Sloss inquiry was over the paediatricians were fighting for their professional lives.

Notes

1 Louis Blom-Cooper, *A Child In Trust: The Protection of Children in a Responsible Society*, Greenwich Borough

Council, 1987. Stephen Sedley, *Whose Child?*, Lambeth Borough Council, 1987.

2   Linda Gordon, *Heroes of Their Own Lives*, New York, 1988.

3   Suzanne Franzway, 'State Action on Sexual Violence', in S. Franzway, D. Court and R.W. Connell, *Staking A Claim: Feminism, Bureaucracy and the State*, Sydney, 1988.

4   *ibid*.

5   The *Sunday Times*, 29 May 1988.

WHAT IS TO BE DONE

Reporting back

Middlesbrough Town Hall had seen nothing like it. None of the chamber's indigenous assemblies carried such frisson as the publication of the Butler-Sloss report on 6 July 1988. The press packed the outer circles of the chamber. A coterie of parents, mainly mothers, held up newspapers in front of their faces to shield themselves from the photographers who jostled in front of the judge's throne, awaiting her arrival – set to be synchronised with Health Minister Tony Newton's speech in the Commons. Everyone was there, except for the three participants most vulnerable to media criticism – Drs Higgs and Wyatt and Sue Richardson.

While professionals working on sexual abuse were kept on hold in the months before publication of the report, the media once again set the terms of the post-publication debate with an unnerving prelude: wild predictions that the paediatricians would be proved wrong vied with what turned out to be accurate predictions that the diagnosis, as a diagnosis, would be vindicated. The former nonetheless loitered like a ghost around the reception of the report: the problem for most of the media was not society's crisis in confronting sexual abuse, but the tragedy of innocent parents wrongly accused. And so the issue was not the difficulty of prevention and detection of the most elusive crime, but the etiquette of intervention.

The report itself was a tactical intervention: most importantly, it acknowledged that sexual abuse of children was a serious social problem demanding subtle co-operation among everyone assigned the responsibility of caring for children. After Lord Justice Butler-Sloss made her carefully enunciated speech which criticised the management of the Cleveland crisis and cautiously exonerated the diagnosis, she left. 'It's a whitewash,' murmured one of the parents as everyone trooped out. That same afternoon in the House of Commons, one of North-Eastern England's three women MPs, Hilary Armstrong, drew a different inference: most of the children involved in the crisis could have been abused, she concluded.

The inquiry and the report did not venture beyond the matter of management. The boundaries around its brief shaped the report's strength and its weakness: it proposed a cold, technocratic modernisation of procedures. Its concern was the response to sexual abuse, not the cause nor the effects. It did not ask why children are abused, nor what it is about our sexual culture that produces sexual abuse. No evidence was sought from perpetrators, nor from professionals working with them, nor from the web of rape crisis centres created during the previous decade to service the survivors of sexual crimes. A sexual crisis became a management crisis and politics became procedures.

The core of the report concerned the behaviour of the social services, the police and the doctors and their treatment of parents and children. But it set the scene with a

What Is To Be Done?

brief history of the attempts since 1985 to modernise procedures, and showed that all the relevant agencies *except the police* had 'become increasingly aware that their existing guidelines offered no assistance to those working in the newly emergent field of child sexual abuse'. The three issues facing them were: who should medically examine children, where should they be examined, and what is the 'propriety and practicality' of the police and social services jointly or co-operatively investigating suspected cases. While affirming the early efforts to deal with child sexual abuse, the report showed that the operational police officers directly concerned with sexual abuse, who worked well with their colleagues in social services, supported the shift toward joint investigation. The CID replaced community relations officers on the working party preparing new guidelines and rejected moves apparently agreed towards joint work, which was seen as a 'curtailment of the right of the police to independent action'.

The report was firm: 'There was a fundamental difference of approach and perspective between the views of some senior officers and other agencies.' There had been 'good progress' which was 'set back' by 'decisions taken by senior officers without wider consultation and which were presented to others as force policy'. These officers, said the report, were unaware of the reasons for changes in procedures based on the protection of children endangered by neglect, violence or torture. 'The police had little experience of the problem of sexual abuse of very young children and they were not aware of the extent to which the representatives of Social Services, Health and voluntary agencies on the working party had moved in their recognition of the problems of child sexual abuse.'

That was the report's assessment of the background to the breakdown in relations between the professionals. So, the eye of the storm was not so much a general failure of inter-agency co-operation, as it came to be represented, as the refusal of the police managers to heed not only the other agencies but also their own operational officers. And that was the background that made sense of the crisis which consumed everyone in 1987.

The police

The report's discussion of the police chronicles the dilemma faced by just such an operational officer, Superintendent Charles Saunders. A regular participant in the working party to reform the guidelines in the couple of years before the crisis, he expressed the belief that the police should act 'as partners in a multi-agency response'. No one listened. 'We heard no evidence that the views of Mr Saunders were ever acknowledged by senior officers,' concluded the report. It went further: 'With the exception of Mr Saunders, we heard little evidence that the Force had recognised or considered in depth the complexities of child sexual abuse, especially the sexual abuse of a child of such tender years as to be unable to give evidence in a criminal court. We were given little confidence that the Force had been willing or committed to dealing with the problem of child sexual abuse, even before the arrival of the Social Services Child Abuse Consultant in 1986.' Nor were the police managers aware of Home Office requirements on procedures for resolving disputes between agencies. All this led to a 'failure to consider and understand the complexities' involved, which in turn led to 'an entrenched stand to resist change'. Their resistance was compounded by their hostility to the 'very strong-willed and determined' Sue Richardson. The report did not comment on why a strong-willed woman was a problem for the police.

What Is To Be Done?

During the crisis the police 'felt that social workers did not understand the constraints upon the police in conducting joint investigations and instigating criminal proceedings'. But the report added that 'the police took no positive and constructive steps to improve understanding by social workers and paediatricians of the difficulties facing the police'. The report shared some of the police concern with the conduct of videoed interviews of children: 'we were convinced that these were not likely to be acceptable in court.' But it concluded that 'the police failed to give sufficient weight' to social services' responsibilities to act on the diagnosis. At stake was the need for mutual support amidst diverging priorities: there are less stringent standards of proof in juvenile courts and in wardship proceedings, where child protection is the priority, than in the criminal courts where the purpose is prosecution.

The report explains that the police were faced with real difficulties when the traditional route of referral – a complaint by a child or another adult – was reversed and diagnosis came before disclosure. As the crisis came to swallow the doctors' time, the police felt frustrated by delays in receiving doctors' statements from the hospital and appeared to be unaware of the practice in other areas, where police went to hospitals to take statements.

'In time, in the minds of investigating officers the lack of further evidence cast doubt on the diagnosis itself,' said the report, and they became reluctant to make arrests based on medical evidence alone. However, it adds that, 'the police appeared to be unaware that the suspicion was raised in many cases by other agencies and referred to Drs Higgs and Wyatt for physical examination'. These were the issues that 'remained unresolved and substantially contributed to the breakdown of relations'.

Then there was the row about photographs of the anus

when it dilated. The police refused to take pictures on the grounds that they recorded no injury and nothing of evidential value. Det. Insp. Alan Walls was dispatched to Dr Higgs to express the views of the Force Scientific Aids Department. 'Having seen Mr Walls in the witness box, his visit to Dr Higgs was clearly more in the nature of a confrontation than an effort to achieve greater mutual understanding.' The report concluded that while 'we have no doubt that police photographers were upset', their boycott was 'supported by their senior officers in circumstances which had no sound basis or support in Force instructions or policy'. All this reinforced the police picture of Dr Higgs. Their suspicions about the efficacy of the diagnosis were guided by their police surgeon, Dr Irvine, and the police came to believe that there was 'a considerable body of eminent medical opinion which disagrees with Dr Higgs' diagnosis'. That body included Dr Irvine, who the police feared was being excluded from examinations. By the end of June, after they had decided to treat the diagnosis with caution, the police issued a press release declaring Dr Irvine had been excluded and that Sue Richardson and Dr Higgs had issued new and substantially different guidelines.

But the report concluded that there were no approved guidelines, that Dr Higgs had played no part in the preparation of the guidelines, and that the press statement 'did nothing to dampen the disagreement between the agencies'. The police had 'received strong encouragement for their reservations from Dr Irvine', which led them to become 'inflexible in their insistence on the use of a police surgeon and Dr Irvine in particular'.

The report offered a damning summary of the symbiotic relationship between the constabulary and the police surgeons. Dr Irvine announced on Tyne Tees Television at

the end of June that Dr Higgs was 'absolutely' wrong and
that 'there was no evidence of abuse on those children'.
But the inquiry found that his evidence was 'confused and
confusing' and he was inexperienced in detecting anal
abuse. 'His strongly held views and emotional behaviour
did not help', and 'unfortunately his views were strongly
reinforced and to some extent formed by his conversations with Dr Roberts, who was far from neutral'.
According to the report, Dr Irvine 'occasionally expressed
his opinions without all the available information and in
ignorance of the wider issues of child sexual abuse. He
did not appear to have advised the police to seek an outside and independent medical opinion. On the contrary,
he encouraged them in their stand. He bears a measure of
responsibility for the troubled relationships between the
police and the Social Services department, and the lack of
balance in some of the media coverage.' He was not alone
in finding the problem of sexual abuse difficult, and
appeared 'to have adopted a position where his examination was unlikely to support an allegation or complaint'.
The police were asking for a second opinion from Dr
Irvine 'to confirm, or, as must have been increasingly obvious in the light of Dr Irvine's declared views, to discount
the diagnosis'. Not only did he reject symptoms regarded
by other doctors as significant, but he 'became emotionally
and personally involved in a way that compromised his
professional position'.

Dr Raine Roberts was an important witness. She was
experienced in the field of sexual abuse and she was Dr
Irvine's mentor. But the inquiry felt that her experience of
anal abuse was 'slight'. She was now faced with a diagnosis 'that she had not previously considered in her practice'.
Either she had been missing a great number of cases over
the years or the paediatricians were wrong. The inquiry

was worried that in some of the cases she examined, 'non-physical indications of a worrying nature were masked by her strongly expressed comments in the reports provided to the parents for court proceedings that there was no medical evidence of sexual abuse'. Furthermore, her language was felt to be over the top, and 'took her outside the role of impartial witness traditionally required of police surgeons. Clearly there are dangers to the police service and the legal system as a whole of such a development.'

Her widely reported allegation that children had been subjected to outrageous abuse by doctors was 'not borne out by the investigations of the Official Solicitor of the children he represented', but Dr Roberts had not recanted. The report concluded that Dr Roberts 'appeared to have become associated with the cause of the parents and was unable to provide us with the cool, detached and considered testimony the inquiry might have expected of the expert, particularly a police surgeon'.

These, then, were the doctors upon whom the police relied in their repudiation of the paediatricians and social workers.

More positively, the report acknowledged that the police tried to rise to the occasion by setting up a specialist child abuse unit at Yarm in the summer of 1987. But it criticised the police for haste and, once again for their lack of consultation with more experienced professionals. 'We heard no evidence of discussions with Social Services or other outside agencies.' Nor was there contact with the specialist Children's Resource Centre at Middlesbrough General, 'an omission which appeared surprising to us'. By setting up a centralised unit, the community relations department lost some of its experienced officers, and long-standing personal-professional relationships on the ground were sacrificed by setting up 'a more distant central office'. The report also expressed surprise that the new unit seemed to have been set up without any new ideas. Police management did not think it necessary 'to reflect new thinking in terms of police relationships with other agencies', and there was caution about 'the value of developments elsewhere'. As the crisis came to a head, the police still 'concentrated their thoughts on the problems of prosecution' rather than child protection, and 'on the conflict over the diagnosis. In doing so they lost sight of the duty to protect children'.

The inquiry team reported that although 'the police tell us that they now accept unequivocally the principle of joint investigation' and co-operation with other professionals, the panel remained sceptical about this *volte face*. It believed that it was only the crisis that 'forced the police somewhat reluctantly into a multi-disciplinary stance' and yet it still felt 'by no means convinced that the implications are either understood or accepted at all levels throughout the force, including the unit at Yarm'.

The doctors and the diagnosis

Given the moral panic which surrounded the mysteries of anal dilatation during 1987, it is noteworthy that the inquiry team in its report supported not the critics of the diagnosis but its advocates, albeit with the cautionary note shared by Drs Wynne and Hobbs, that it should be considered in the context of other signs and symptoms.

Far from endorsing the view of Dr Roberts and Basingstoke's Dr Heald that it was 'normal', the inquiry shared the view of the overwhelming majority of medical witnesses that the sign, while not proof of anal abuse, should arouse suspicion. Contrary to its view of Dr Roberts' evidence, it found Dr Wynne's evidence 'helpful' and accepted the consensus, expressed by the British

Paediatric Association and the Police Surgeons Association, that the sign should alert doctors to suspicions of sexual abuse.

The inquiry reported that before the crisis erupted there were already some acrimonious feelings towards Drs Higgs and Wyatt among senior doctors, managers and members of the Community Health Council, which later became intensely critical of their sexual abuse strategy. Drs Higgs and Wyatt had complained to the District Medical Advisory Committee about resource cuts and 'asset stripping in the paediatric services', adapting their complaint from an earlier paper jointly written with Dr Morrell entitled 'Skimping on the Care of the Newborn'. This paper touched a raw nerve: Britain in the 1980s saw a rise in infant mortality and a decline in its ranking with other European countries in the care of babies. Dr Higgs was expected to specialise in the care of babies and apparently irritated managers by her additional interest in sexual abuse as a health hazard. The number of sexual abuse diagnoses can, however, be better understood as a proportion of the total number of children seen by the doctors. Between January and July 1987, Drs Higgs and Wyatt saw a total of 2,306 outpatients and diagnosed sexual abuse in 77 index children (the first in a family to be diagnosed – the remainder of the total of 121 diagnoses involved siblings, and so on).

The report affirmed both doctors as diligent and caring and recalled letters sent to the inquiry by nurses saying, 'We have seen in her the same level of care and dedication as always shown by Dr Wyatt', and by the public saying, 'Keep on doing what you believe is right, keep on trying to stop child abuse.' But the report also criticised Dr Higgs for failing to appreciate that she was in a leadership position and that she should 'provide local guidelines to help nurses cope with a new problem'. The inquiry felt that Dr Higgs 'was unaware of the importance' of taking responsibility for 'the marked distress and general upset of the nursing staff'. Despite several attempts to arrange meetings with nursing officers, 'she was either late or did not arrive at all'.

Her management of cases was based on the physical abuse model, designed to protect a child in peril – an approach which prompted criticism from both paediatricians and social services. Although some professionals' techniques in interviewing children were subject to stiff criticism during the inquiry, it reported that it had seen a video of Dr Higgs interviewing a child and 'we were very impressed'.

The report's criticism focused on two themes: Dr Higgs' certainty about her diagnosis, and her refusal to heed her colleagues' advice that she should proceed more strategically and slowly. Her trajectory seemed to have been set, said the report, by some early successes, when her diagnosis was confirmed. The inquiry did not believe, however, that she routinely examined children for sexual abuse. She conducted her examinations only if there was already something to arouse her suspicion. Furthermore, 'it was only rarely that she relied exclusively upon anal dilatation as the only physical sign. There is no doubt however that she relied heavily upon the sign in support of her diagnosis.'

Given the widespread predictions that the diagnosis would be discredited, it is significant that the report states: 'we have in general no reason to doubt her clinical observations.' The inquiry's criticism was less concerned with medical signs than with management: 'it was the certainty of the conclusions drawn from the findings which was open to criticism' and which did not give 'an opportunity for others such as social workers to obtain wider assessment of the family'. Dr Higgs 'showed an inability to understand the point of view of others or appreciate their difficulties during the crisis', and her 'obvious ability to deal with children and empathise with them did not extend to parents'. Many of the criticisms of Dr Higgs' management extended to Dr Wyatt, who was not represented in the report as the rather awed, subordinate character portrayed in the media. 'In much of the evidence and in the media Dr Higgs has appeared the more dominant personality, but the dedication, single-minded enthusiasm and determination of Dr Wyatt was a considerable factor at this time and they supported each other in their work.'

Social services

If anything it was the social services department which drew the inquiry's special sting. Despite its caution against scapegoating, and its plea that social workers be supported in their child protection work, the report pointed the finger of blame at Sue Richardson and her director Mike Bishop. The report made it clear that the process of reforming inappropriate guidelines was inaugurated before Sue Richardson's appointment and renewed after it. It seemed to reproduce the representation of her as a problem.

While accepting that many of the parents' criticisms of social workers were understandable, the report situated the social services department's response to the sexual abuse overload in the context of growing public anxiety about the failure to protect children whose lives and well-being had been palpably imperilled within their families. It contrasted the department's careful consideration of individual cases before 1987, its calculations about the proximity of the abuser and the capacity of the mother to protect her children before removing them, with the department's practices in 1987. 'Social workers and their managers were anxious not to have been seen to fail the children involved by leaving them in situations of risk,' it said. Since the paediatricians were diagnosing the most gross forms of abuse, social workers, who did not feel competent to make judgements about the diagnosis, 'felt obliged to follow the diagnosis and take steps to protect the child'. Their actions were not only determined by that imperative but by the consultants' pressure to take place of safety orders. This produced an 'immediate emergency intervention' which failed to recognise that child sexual abuse has different characteristics from physical abuse and annihilated the opportunity for assessment of each case. Furthermore, the report took a dim view of social services managers and Sue Richardson when they 'suspended disbelief' in the possibility that abuse had not taken place. Although the report accepted that Cleveland 'has been trying to maintain a high standard of service to families and children in desperately difficult circumstances', it concluded that the suspension of disbelief was 'not a helpful approach'.

The social workers' difficulty was compounded, however, both by the police, who were 'reluctant to investigate possible perpetrators', and by Dr Higgs' failure to deliver speedy statements. This put a premium on place of safety orders, not so much to secure protection but to 'control parental access and in order to facilitate disclosure interviews with children'. The diagnosis needed a disclosure.

Director Mike Bishop was an experienced manager who, it seems unlike his police counterpart, had 'kept himself up to date with developments in the child care field' and resolved that his department would learn from mistakes elsewhere which left children to their abusers. At the beginning of June he called in the paediatricians and gave them the third degree. They convinced him of the validity of the diagnosis. As the swathe of referrals swamped the department and the diagnosis became increasingly contested by parents, he called in the DHSS Inspectorate for advice. By mid-June he 'took urgent steps to establish arrangements for second opinions' and set up a special child abuse group to monitor and co-ordinate the response to the diagnosis. By the end of the month, Bishop swiftly set up the Children's Resource Centre and sought a meeting with his police counterpart, Chief Constable Payne. In the wake of his own department's decision to act on the diagnosis, and the police decision to do the opposite, it was an unfruitful exchange. Despite all his efforts, the report criticises him and his headquarters for their failure to shorten the lines of management, to alert elected councillors to the controversial nature of the diagnosis, and to seek advice outside Cleveland, and for trying to cope by 'addressing logistical issues rather than taking control'. Mike Bishop accepted the device of taking place of safety orders while investigations proceeded, but this kind of control 'led to a peremptory use of authority which alienated parents and made the proper task of social workers impractical, that is to say the carrying out of a full assessment of the family'. The clear implication is that he should have called a halt to the paediatricians and diverted his adviser Sue Richardson from her commitment to her colleagues in the hospital.

Curiously, Mike Bishop is implicitly criticised for believing the diagnosis and then acting on it, albeit with a blunt instrument. His were largely sins of commission, compounded by loyalty to colleagues whose specialisms he trusted. He was operating within antique structures in the absence of their modernisation, which had largely been thwarted by the police. None of the vehemence of the report's criticisms was matched by the report's treatment of Bishop's opposite number in the Cleveland constabulary, Chief Constable Christopher Payne. His were largely sins of omission and of opposition to the views of those officers with operational skills in sexual abuse work. Mike Bishop is named and blamed for trying to do something. Payne is barely mentioned, perhaps because he tried to do nothing.

Bishop is also criticised for relying too heavily on Sue Richardson, an experienced and respected social worker who saw sexual abuse as 'a unique constellation of trauma'. Throughout the report she is described as determined, strong-willed and a woman with firm views. Just like Lord Justice Butler-Sloss. But while these qualities were celebrated in the judge, whose control of the inquiry was tempered by wit and a gleam in her eye, in Richardson, whose appearance at the inquiry was constrained by an overly defensive strategy by her legal team, they seemed to produce alienation. Sue Richardson believed that social workers needed 'an authoritative base' from which to counter an abuser's misuse of power, and she told the inquiry that, like others in her field, she now felt that 'the policy of investigating sexual abuse by family co-operation is a bit of a myth'. What this position did not acknowledge – and neither did the report – were the different positions of mothers and fathers.

Sue Richardson was also criticised for going into the crucial 28 May meeting with the police with 'confrontation' rather than conciliation in mind, despite the evidence that the police officers arrived ill prepared and determined to stick by their man, Dr Irvine. The report appeared to reproduce the stereotype of a strong woman who was not so much authoritative as authoritarian.

Psychological services

The report concluded that the area's Department of Child and Adolescent Psychiatry was not in a position to offer the North Tees District's clinical psychologist, Heather Bacon, who bore much of the brunt of the crisis, 'the kind of professional support she was in need of'. This was because of the department's referral system being restricted to medical channels, and because of the views of the department. Dr Chisholm was unhappy with techniques used in interviews with children and Dr Wignarajah was concerned about separating children suspected of having been abused from their parents. One of the effects of these differences was that paediatricians in Cleveland preferred to send children to psychiatrists elsewhere. Heather Bacon was left 'isolated and unsupported', according to the report, which nevertheless criticised her for failing to separate the 'evaluative phase' from the 'therapeutic phase' – a clear criticism of the tendency to work on the assumption that abuse had taken place. While criticising her interviewing techniques in one case, the report concluded that videos of some interviews showed that she had 'a kindly, sensitive approach to children'. The report made no comment on the paucity of therapeutic services in the National Health Service for either children or adults, victims or their abusers.

The courts

The practice during the Cleveland crisis of seeking care orders from court officers out of working-time was criticised by the report, which recommended stringent record-keeping and monitoring by juvenile and magistrates courts, as well as the shift towards shorter place of safety orders. The report endorsed the wide support for a specialist Family Court, and proposed a new government department, an Office of Child Protection.

Training

If Cleveland came out of the crisis and the inquiry with criticism on all sides, the report nonetheless implicitly recognised the poverty of specialist skills available in Britain when it strongly recommended that the education of everyone involved in the care of children should receive instruction on child sexual abuse. Once in work they should receive in-service training, too. There should also be specialised training for those working with families in which sexual abuse is suspected. The police and social workers should have joint training, given the need for inter-agency co-operation. Paediatricians should be trained in evidential requirements. In a comment typical of the report's tone of 'common sense', it urged that everyone working in the field 'must have an empathy with children and "their feet on the ground"'.

The government, on the day of publication, supported this approach, and recommended that the police, local government and health authorities consider setting up specialist teams, already in post in a few areas. It offered an extra £7 million to be spent in 1989 by local authorities to help train social workers in child abuse work – only a few weeks after it had rejected an appeal for £40 million needed to extend social work training to three years. The depths of the economic crisis facing social services had already been revealed by social services directors, who reported that there were 4000 job vacancies. In London alone, according to the Social Services Inspectorate, there were 600 cases of children known to be at risk of all forms of abuse who had not been allocated to the care of any social worker.

Stuart Bell

The Middlesbrough MP's allegations of empire-building by Cleveland's social services – eccentric in the light of this national crisis – were rejected by the report, which also repudiated his allegation of conspiracy between Dr Higgs and Sue Richardson. Contrary to his claim that the social services department had launched a 'fundamental attack on family life', it believed that although social services worked with inappropriate place of safety orders, social workers 'had acted with the highest motives' and 'we are equally satisfied that at no time was there an intention to make a fundamental attack on family life'. Dealing with his dossier of cases, the report concluded that 'not all the information given to Mr Bell was accurate and some was misleading'.

All this amounts to a benign but devastating critique. But the report, which did not hesitate elsewhere to point the finger of blame, remained curiously coy about the Cleveland constabulary management's culpability. Perhaps more important, it was silent about the political implications of its criticisms. For the first time, however, the County Council's politicians acted with élan. Despite the report's counsel: no scapegoats, a group of councillors recommended exactly that – that Mike Bishop and Sue Richardson be purged. This provoked criticism from other councillors and was fiercely resisted by Town Hall trade unionists.

The imponderable remained Cleveland constabulary, apparently a law unto itself. Why did the report not hold Chief Constable Christopher Payne responsible for his management's truculent inertia and its failure to endorse the wisdoms of officers like Supt. Saunders? Why did it not ask to whom and how the police could be made accountable to its community? And why did it not discuss the implications of the behaviour of the police and the police surgeons? What, we are entitled to wonder, should we think of court cases conducted during the life of the inquiry in which the evidence of the police surgeons carried such weight? Were those children sexually abused, and if they were, how could they be safe? The effect of the campaign against the paediatricians and social services left them beyond the reach of relief.

Right is wrong – secret document keeps the secret

The evidence before the inquiry from eminent paediatricians confirming the significance of the contested sign might have reassured the regional health authority, which had consulted the paediatricians during the crisis and accepted their clinical judgement. But it did not. As a consensus emerged in support of the sign, marked by the near-unanimity of the British Paediatric Association and the Police Surgeons Association, the inquiry drifted in a different direction. The further the inquiry strayed from that suggestive sign, the more precarious became the paediatricians' position.

The dissenters had to discredit the sign. They failed. The conviction among the paediatricians and the employers was that if the paediatricians were right in about three-quarters of their diagnoses they would be safe. But instead of that consensus increasing the confidence of the employers in the paediatricians, goodwill ebbed as summer became autumn, and autumn turned to winter. By December the talk among them was chilling – the diagnosis didn't matter and the doctors would get done on their filing, their manners, anything.

It was obvious in 1988 that the paediatricians were doomed despite the fact that the Butler-Sloss report said it did not doubt their clinical findings. So, were they right? They may have been right but their *political* judgement about resource management was now what was deemed wrong. The Butler-Sloss report did not criticise the resource managers. It only criticised the clinicians.

The clearest confirmation of the strength of the diagnosis is to be found in a confidential report that was never shared with the public and, therefore, never allowed to influence either the public debate or resource priorities. It was prepared by the managers of the Northern Regional Health Authority in October 1988, and sent to the Department of Health. *Action Taken Following the Report of the Judicial Inquiry into Child Abuse in Cleveland* confirmed that, after consulting the professional community, the accuracy of the paediatricians' diagnosis had been found to be 'arguably better than might be achieved in other fields of medicine at the stage of initial observation'. So, here was a higher-than-average rate of diagnostic accuracy. 'The true figure will never be known and the Butler-Sloss Report makes no attempt to estimate it,' notes the NRHA report, but '*it is clear that there was no wholesale error of diagnosis*' (my italics). And yet the entire story started with the dissidents' confident belief that the diagnosis was wrong.

Detailing the outcome of contested cases involving second opinions the NRHA has this to say: 'Some light is thrown on this by the investigations of the Independent Panel and the Regional Reference Group set up by the Regional Medical Officer. The Independent Panel, 'comprising eminent paediatricians and child psychiatrists from outside and within the region and working in pairs, undertook extremely thorough and in-depth assessments of the children and families'. They confirmed that in 25 out of 29 children the diagnosis was confirmed or there was strong cause for concern. Among the children seen by the Regional Reference Group, 14 out of 22 cases were confirmed.

The figure these professionals came up with was 70–75 per cent correct diagnoses. If the collective view was right then 'it would clearly be contrary to general public understanding of the accuracy of the diagnoses'. But the NRHA did nothing to enlighten the public. Nor did the Department of Health.

Their silence told us something significant. Trailing the Butler-Sloss Report's implicit conclusion that even if the diagnosis was correct it didn't matter, that the children had been harmed not so much by the sexual crimes committed against them as by the mode of intervention, the NRHA report concluded that, although the paediatricians were not responsible for the intervention, their diagnosis was. Their administrative and social shortcomings were 'not uncommon in everyday medical practice'. The paediatricians were deemed 'conscientious' and 'competent' and Dr Wyatt was regarded by patients with 'an attitude of devotion', said the report. But none of this mattered.

Undoubtedly, their practice of immediately sharing their concern with the parents often produced instant polarisation, which gave the professionals little room to manoeuvre, to make a plan. But involving the parents was a principal recommendation of the Butler-Sloss Report, so perhaps that didn't matter either. A local childcare manager said later, 'Looking back, informing parents would inevitably cause difficulties because that meant possibly telling an alleged abuser. We soon learned that the helpful thing for the child was to involve the non-abusing parent, usually the mother. But since Cleveland and the Children Act, however, the irony is that we are encouraged to do

what Dr Higgs and Dr Wyatt did. What they did out of
naivety or goodwill, we have to do because of political
pressure. We not only involve parents, but parents convicted of serious offences against their children. Either
way, we know this often silences children.'

There were massive resource implications. The paediatricians had long complained about work-house conditions
and skimping on services for children. By any standard,
children's health services in Cleveland were woeful and
what the diagnosis had exposed was a resource crisis.
Their refusal to retreat from their clinical duty was deemed
a 'serious failure of judgement' – precisely because they
exposed that resource crisis and the failure of health service managers to respond to it.

That was what produced a severe reprimand at the end
of the year. Dr Higgs and Dr Wyatt were banned from
doing any direct work with sexual abuse. Cruelly, Dr Higgs
was removed to Tyneside.

Would the NRHA have cried 'serious failure of judgement' if the paediatricians had turned away children
suffering from asthma attacks or meningitis? Well, in 1988
it might not have dared. But several years after the crisis,
health service managers were willing to say as much when
the ban on the doctors was re-imposed, despite many paediatricians' protests. To go on challenging managers about
resources was enough reason, apparently, to be punished
in perpetuity.

The managers' dread of another 'child abuse controversy' implied – ironically – its inevitability.

Professionals confronting childhood sexual abuse are
'at the crux of a historic contest', warns the California
clinician Roland Summit, one of the most influential advocates for the victims and a veteran of many child abuse
cases in the US.[1]

'This is about woundings and casualties caused not by bacteria or viruses, but perpetrated by people', comments a child protection specialist in Britain, Judith Dawson Jones. 'Symptoms are signs of injury caused by someone – that is bound to be contested; it is inevitably going to be a war zone. Unless organisations understand and prepare for the implications and issues at every level, by being explicit about how they will support and manage staff and clients, the children's service will be insecure. Children will have yet another experience of not being protected. Remember what the perpetrator will have made them feel: no one will believe you – I am the most powerful person in your world.'

Parents in about half the cases involved initiated legal proceedings against the doctors. They believed these claims could be resisted, but the new arrangements for NHS indemnity introduced in 1990 took the decision away from them and gave responsibility for negligence claims to the health authorities – the employers. In 1991, without admitting liability, the NRHA settled the claims out of court for a reported £1 million. Parents who believed the diagnosis received none of it. The perceived public message was: Hah! The doctors got it wrong.

However, no complaints were ever made to the doctors' regulator, the General Medical Council.

Secrets, lies and videotape

What did this great controversy leave behind? It told us that nothing is more important than keeping the secret of sexual abuse.

When it decided to hold an inquiry into Cleveland, the government decided to investigate only the arrangements. It evaded the question: what had been happening to these children, what the sign meant and what we should do when the sign is shadowed by silence.

We need go no further than Lord Butler-Sloss herself for an eloquent exegesis. Were the children abused or not? 'It was not my job to find out,' she told a meeting of the Medico-Legal Society in March 1989, 'I do not know how many children were abused in Cleveland.' She criticised practitioners who worked on the assumption that there had been abuse, and criticised the resort to devices like anatomically correct dolls to help children describe their experiences. After all professionals were trying everything to help children speak about the unspeakable. 'It's a cheek, really,' commented one social services manager. 'I wonder if this judge has ever sat with a tortured six-year-old who has to speak to a stranger for her own safety, but can't.' With little of the gracious gravitas an audience might expect of a judge, Butler-Sloss mocked those 'appallingly misnamed' dolls thus: 'May I tell you that the Women's Institute of Somerset have been knitting them! (Laughter) If nothing else, we really ought to keep those particularly hideous dolls away from most children.'[2]

The inquiry began with a sign that suggested sexual abuse, but, as she reminded us, it was not her job to determine whether or not children had been abused: 'My job was to look at the arrangements.' But how could the inquiry sensibly assess the appropriate arrangements if the government had decided *not to know* whether the children had been abused?

Clearly, intervention was contingent on investigation and the work of interpretation. Society could only know whether children had been abused through 'detection or admission'. But the police had detonated detection. That left intervention dependent on the doctors' interpretation of the sign. The arrangements could not be considered without an assessment of the sign – they had to go together.

The inquiry accepted the medical consensus: in general, the sign was serious and suggestive, if not conclusive. The inquiry could not have been unaware of the medical consensus in the particular Cleveland cases. But by separating the general from the particular, it was relieved of responsibility for assessing the crux of the crisis: what is society supposed to do when a sign strongly suggestive of sexual abuse is accompanied by silence? 'One of the extraordinary elements about Cleveland was that there were relatively few children who told a story,' she told her colleagues.

But the inquiry did not extend its gaze from the problem of the sign to the resolution of the problem of silence. What it did do was focus on the dependence on disclosure – by the perpetrator or the victim – created by the impossibility of detection.

Just as the whole inquiry was a response to the dissent from the diagnosis, so it was propelled by the dissidents when it shifted its gaze away from the sign to the difficulty of disclosure. It recoiled from the compelling matrix of signs and silences, and reproached the professionals left struggling with the sound of silence. 'It is important to recall that sexual abuse exists, but by and large in Cleveland the children did not tell us so, and we must not push children into giving accounts in a way that puts too much pressure on them,' Butler-Sloss said in 1989.

At this point it is worth returning to those months in 1987 when the inquiry was hearing evidence from the experts. No expert was invited to give evidence on the pressure put on children by perpetrators. But in Britain and the United States practitioners working with perpetrators were already alerting the professional community to the perpetrators' strategies designed to secure silence.

The inquiry heard evidence from only one American expert, Dr Ralph Underwager, an assiduous advocate for accused adults. We didn't know it then but we do know now just how central he was to the 'historic contest' over signs, silence and speech in the drama of sexual oppression. Had it not welcomed Underwager, we could have imagined that the inquiry was acting naively, but it should have known that it was viewing evidence from an activist in a great debate, who made his name as a campaigner for accused adults and as a ubiquitous critic of one of his country's most respected advocates for abused children and adults, Dr Roland Summit.

Summit's great contribution to the debates was his poignant essay on strategic silence, 'The Child Sexual Abuse Accommodation Syndrome'.[3] Dr Summit is a community physician in California, and also a clinical associate professor, with a history in psychoanalysis, whose modest hospital office is covered with awards from his peers. He proposed a way of thinking about children's agency in the context of abuse. That agency was expressed not in the vaunted fantasy and fabrication hypotheses of the Freudian medical establishment – repeated, ironically by the anti-Freudian Underwager – but in tactics of accommodation.

The pastor

The prelude to Underwager's appearance in Middlesbrough on 14 December was a rehearsal of his evidence in the *Daily Mail*. It was an inauspicious start. Lord Butler-Sloss was not pleased. It was a 'most flagrant breach' said the judge, who did not like reading in the newspaper 'what the valuable and important witness who has crossed the Atlantic to come to give evidence to this inquiry has to say to us'. Furthermore, 'this inquiry is not to be used as a platform'.

Underwager is a Minnesota Lutheran pastor with a psychology degree. He told the inquiry that he and his wife, Hollida Wakefield, became involved in 'false accusations' in 1976. He appeared always for the defence and reckoned that he gave expert testimony in an average of at least one case a week.

His evidence was this:

- There is no evidence that anal abuse is anything but rare. 'Anal assault upon children is possibly the most rare and infrequent of the actual forms of abuse that occur.' When it occurs it requires 'considerable force and results in great trauma and injury'. Digital penetration of the anus 'just does not happen now'. He rejected counsel's suggestion that anal abuse might be attractive to the abuser of a young child because the anus would be easier to penetrate than the vagina. It was contrary to common sense, he said; it carried no reward or reinforcement. 'What kind of person gets their joys out of digital penetration? What is the reinforcement?' he wondered. What is the 'turn-on'?

- Only 5 per cent of original allegations are found to be factual. He drew this inference from the proportion of original allegations that resulted in criminal convictions in the courts. There is a widespread belief that the criminal justice system is the most inhospitable arbiter of allegations of abuse. Underwager, however, said the figure of 5 per cent was taken from the fate of allegations 'that are determined finally by our justice system, the final arbiter of what is factual and what is not'.

- The concern with sexual abuse merely leads to 'false positives' – the assumption that a child has been abused

when it has not. 'For every one person correctly identified as an abuser nine innocent people . . . are
incorrectly identified.'

- 'False positives' are worse than 'false negatives'. 'The
cost of a false negative to the child and to society and to
the family is much less than the cost of a false positive.'

- Child protection professionals lie. Leading questions,
pressure, threats and force, teaching aids, modelling
aids and the reinforcement of responses induce widespread error. Worse, child protection workers and
interviewers, dubbed 'interrogators' by Underwager,
'lie. They threaten. They fabricate.'

- There is no evidence that apparently 'normal' people
abuse children. Asked about abuse in 'otherwise well-
adjusted, effective family settings in which the parents
appear outwardly to be capable, caring, ordinary parents', Underwager insisted that this was not credible,
because sexual abuse was 'outside the boundaries of
normally accepted social behaviour' and if people
strayed beyond those boundaries in one area they
would do so in another.

- There is no evidence that children are blocked or
silenced, or that abuse within families is compulsive or
secretive. 'I know of no research whatsoever that would
support the contention or claim that sexual offences
are compulsive.' There is no scientific evidence for the
notion, supported by Dr Summit, 'that children maintain some kind of secrecy'. The notion that a child
might be blocked 'is pure assumption, pure speculation'.

- There is no point in the 'talking cure'. Asked whether
it would ever benefit a child to 'bottle up these feelings
and this secret', Underwager replied, 'All of the history and research evidence available on therapy with

children shows that there is no therapeutic efficacy to the expression of feelings.'

- Sexual abuse is not as harmful as people think. 'Such abuse, contrary to the popular and much-bruited dogma, is shown by the evidence not to be as harmful as we think it to be . . . it is not as harmful as most would insist that it is.'

Although Underwager cautioned professionals to be alert to their own bias, he was felt by the inquiry panel not to be the best exemplar of his own advice. Nevertheless he was an important witness, whose work provided the ideological rock for the movement of accused adults, Parents Against Injustice (PAIN) in Britain and its equivalent in the US, Victims of the Child Abuse Laws (VOCAL).

When he gave evidence in Cleveland the quality of his evidence in over two hundred cases in the courts in the United States and elsewhere, including Britain, was already so alarming prosecutors in his own country that the New England Commissioners of Child Welfare Agencies commissioned a special study of his writing and his testimony. The author of the study was Anna Salter, a highly respected professional, author of *Treating Child Sex Offenders and Victims: A Practical Guide*, who was first exposed personally to his testimony when he claimed that research showed that 'children are very suggestible'. She checked and discovered that, on the contrary, the research concluded that 'no systematic relationship between age and suggestibility has been consistently documented'. She amassed 500 articles and several books by Underwager and Wakefield, and discovered over a hundred errors in their bibliography alone. Her exhaustive survey uncovered an extraordinary degree of inaccuracy and misrepresentation, but, worse, 'the inaccuracies were uniformly in the service of strengthening W and U's case against children who report child sexual abuse. At best this speaks to extraordinary bias. Were the issue simply sloppy research, one would expect the errors to be randomly distributed.'[4] Legal practitioners confronted by their testimony 'would be well-advised to go back to the original sources and check the accuracy of that testimony before accepting it'. This was too late for the Cleveland inquiry.

Dr Salter's devastating critique contains an interesting appendix which illuminates some of the methods used by Underwager and Wakefield. In 1988 they addressed a conference of defence attorneys in Nashville, Tennessee, which was attended by Dr Salter and several other mental health professionals who challenged their statistics.

A few weeks later, Dr Salter was telephoned by a woman purporting to be the mother of a child alleging abuse and asking her to testify. Dr Salter refused. Asked about Underwager, she commented that he always appeared for the defence and mentioned her concerns about his scholarship. A week later the transcript of this conversation arrived in the post – from Underwager. He hinted at legal action and announced that Ms Wakefield was taking a charge of ethics violation to the American Psychological Association. In July 1989 the APA's Ethics Committee voted unanimously to 'dismiss the complaint as entirely without merit'. On another occasion, Underwager and Wakefield sued Salter and Patricia Toth, director of the National Center for Prosecution of Child Abuse, for defamation. The case was dismissed and in April 1994 the appeal, too, was dismissed.

In the 1990s Underwager helped to launch the False Memory Syndrome Foundation, which extended his authority as an advocate for accused adults in VOCAL to an offshoot, a movement of adults accused by their *adult* children of sexual abuse: the FMSF emerged among parents who sought help from Underwager and Wakefield's Institute for Psychological Therapies in Minnesota.

Perhaps emboldened by the palpable success of the backlash against children's evidence which he had diligently served, in 1993 he came out in support of paedophilia in a candid interview with the Dutch journal of paedophilia, *Paedika*.

Underwager comments that paedophilia, like other sexual orientations, is a choice, and 'paedophiles can boldly and courageously affirm what they choose. They can say what they want is the best way to love. I am also a theologian and as a theologian I believe it is God's will that there be closeness and intimacy, unity of the flesh between people. A paedophile can say: "This closeness is possible for me within the choices I have made."

'With boldness they can say: "I believe this is in fact part of God's will." They have the right to make these statements: "I believe that God's will is that we have absolute freedom. No conditions. No contingencies."'

Hollida Wakefield intervenes with a caution: 'Speaking about men and boys at least, what I have seen is that once the young man gets to a certain age the paedophile is no longer interested.' How could a relationship progress, she wondered, since paedophilia was inherently about youth, and that problem was compounded by the hostile social climate? Asked what tack paedophiles should take, given that hostility, Underwager proposes that 'paedophiles become much more positive. They should directly attack the concept, the image, the picture of the paedophile as an evil, wicked, and reprehensible exploiter of children.'

Underwager's misogyny starts to show and draws his wife's firm protest when he blames 'radical feminism, which includes a pretty hefty dose of anti-maleness', for 'anti-sexuality outbursts'. He ventures, 'There is a very real way these women may be jealous that males are able to love each other.'

Finally, he returns to *Paedika*'s core concern and counsels paedophiles to 'Take the risk, the consequences of the risk and make the claim: this is something good.'

Confident that their time had come he may have been, but the interview provoked a great row – and his resignation from the FMSF board. Hollida Wakefield remained.

Dr Summit

Since the conundrum that vexed everyone involved in the Cleveland crisis was the silence shrouding physical signs, it was extraordinary that Underwager's great enemy, Roland Summit, was not invited to give evidence – because his work was concerned with precisely that conundrum. His germinal essay 'The Child Sexual Abuse Accommodation Syndrome', published in 1983, proposed five categories: secrecy, helplessness, entrapment and accommodation, delayed and conflicted disclosure and, finally, retraction.

- 'However gentle or menacing the intimidation may be,' suggests Summit, secrecy is both 'the source of fear and the promise of safety' for the victim; and, since a child is not prepared for the possibility of molestation, it is 'entirely dependent on the intruder for whatever reality is assigned to the experience'.
- For the adult world to expect the child to protect itself and expose the offence is to ignore the condition of childhood, the subordination and helplessness that define its relation to the authority of adults. Although children are given permission to reject the attention of

strangers, they are required to be 'obedient and affectionate with any adult entrusted with their care'.

- However racked an abusive adult might feel, the circumstance of secrecy and 'the unexpected ease of accomplishment seem to invite repetition'. Compulsive patterns tend to develop 'until the child achieves autonomy or until discovery'. For a child to imagine a parent as ruthless and selfish 'is tantamount to abandonment and annihilation'. The only alternative is a 'desperate assumption of responsibility and the inevitable failure to earn relief'. The child has the power to 'destroy the family and to keep it together. The child, not the parent, must mobilise the altruism and self-control to insure the survival of others'. Thus, 'the healthy, normal, emotionally resilient child will learn to accommodate the reality of continuing sexual abuse'. Since most abuse is never disclosed, disclosure is 'an outgrowth either of overwhelming family conflict, incidental discovery by a third party' or of sensitive community education.

- And since a child faces 'an unbelieving audience' if it reveals abuse, an alternative accommodation pattern may express itself as an eager-to-please strategy that hides conflict. The way that the criminal justice system receives any complaint from a child may lead to the child's removal from home, while the accused adult is unlikely to be called to account in a criminal court. Even when children's complaints are corroborated by other children, their testimony 'will be impeached by trivial discrepancies'.

- Whatever a child says about sexual abuse, it is 'likely to reverse it'. Behind the action that produces disclosure 'remains the ambivalence of guilt and the martyred obligation to preserve the family'. Dr Summit later comments that a child who is already well-practised in divining what will minimize rejection and conflict' can easily turn to retraction which, of course, is what the adult world wants to hear. The survivor is both blamed and rewarded for retraction. It is what earns the respect and relief of 'distressed sceptics' as well as appeasing the conflicts created 'by incriminating a trusted, often cherished adult'. Unspoken clues are all a child needs to 'keep the peace'.

In a later paper Dr Summit argues that the resistance to children's disclosures – yet another pressure to retract – is compounded by 'overloaded protective resources and community tolerance'.[5]

Dr Summit's challenge to commonsense expectation of exposure is confirmed by Teena Sorensen and Barbara Snow, whose research in Utah among hundreds of children, from toddlers to teenagers, helps to explain the inexplicable: the reluctance to reveal the offence and the striking rate of retraction by children in confirmed cases of sexual abuse (confirmed mostly by an admission). Taking more than a hundred confirmed cases, involving mainly 'middle class' children, Sorensen and Snow map the children's stories and monitor how they stumble and swerve.[6]

Three-quarters of the cases came to the authorities' attention accidentally – often because a known offender was discovered in the child's milieu. More than three-quarters of the children initially denied any abuse. Tentative disclosure then became the most common next step (78 per cent), characterised by confusing, inaccurate and uncertain stories, 'often vacillating from acknowledgement to denial'. More than 20 per cent recanted and finally 93 per cent reaffirmed the allegation of abuse.

What Summit and Sorensen and Snow describe is a

reluctant narrative that moves back and forth, frustrating adults' demands for clarity and certainty while children themselves navigate a lonely journey towards uncertain survival. Sorensen and Snow's chilling conclusion is that 'The only person for whom denial is as great as that of the perpetrator may be the victim.'

These clinicians' humanity is palpable in their patience and modesty. Underwager's bravado appeared to gain little support at the Cleveland inquiry and his position was ultimately revealed in his *Paedika* interview: he is revealed as the champion not of children but of people who want sex with children. Dr Summit, by contrast, starts with children's suffering. He allows himself to be interested in the meanings of their 'bad' and 'good' behaviour, their self-harm and silences, and the futility of protest in a world that has decided to not know.

What on earth made the inquiry want to listen to the one and not the other? Why, when Underwager told the panel about his main enemy, Roland Summit, did it not seek him out? And why did the inquiry not call evidence on the perpetrators who produce both the suffering and the silence? Ray Wyre, a probation officer who set up Britain's first centre specialising in work with sex offenders, did not give evidence. Nor did Steven Wolf, one of the leading US experts on perpetrators, who toured Britain sharing his research in several seminars during the mid-1980s.

The story of Cleveland starts with the body. The clue to the inquiry's interests and its evasions also lie in the body and its meanings. The sign drew attention in a new way both to the offender and to the victim; to the offenders' challenge to conventional wisdoms about heterosexuality as well as to their determined control of the child and its entire environment; and to the victim's agency – not as a seducer but as a survivor.

Cleveland presents us with a medical model that appears to relieve the child of the entire responsibility for an explanation, that treats the injuries suffered by both body and mind like any other injury: as a trauma for the individual that demands both protection and prevention. However, relief brings its own crisis in the child's cosmos. The contested signs tell their own story of speechless accommodation: a body's survival strategy for everyday life that is robust in defeat, the child's body taking responsibility for overpowering intrusion. The signs speak volumes about the silence – the altered architecture of a chronically abused anus *is* the anatomy of accommodation.

Why did the inquiry not take evidence that might help make sense of the Cleveland mystery and its place in the volcanic history of sexual politics: the knot of strong signs and silence? *Why did it decide not to know?*

The arrangements

Chapter 12 of the Cleveland Report is the biblical chapter, the Maastricht Treaty of child protection arrangements. Woe betide any professional who has not read Chapter 12.

This is the chapter that prescribed, for the next decade, the protocols for abused children with a story to tell. This is the chapter that shifts the centre of gravity from the sign to speech, and this is the chapter that, therefore, wrestles with the crisis that occupies the space between signs and silence. What Chapter 12 does not do, however, is liberate the narrative, let the child speak in its own way, its own time, to whomever it chooses. On the contrary, Chapter 12 is concerned with controlling the conditions in which children may speak.[7]

The chapter's first priority is to caution professionals against 'disclosure' work and to warn that adults may malevolently make children disclose fictitious abuse. The tone is clear: children should be taken seriously, but don't assume abuse, and beware bad motives.

Mainstream professionals are contrasted with Underwager, who is accorded the status of a sceptical sage and in the great tournament the pastor, the accused parents' advocate, can feel confident that he has prevailed.

For example, Professor David Jones describes the therapeutic conversations with children designed to support their struggle to speak as 'disclosure work', which he defines as 'a clinically useful concept to describe the process by which a child who has been sexually abused within the family gradually comes to inform the outside world of his/her plight'. Asking, 'Do children lie about or fantasise about it?' Chapter 12 offers three warnings: children may fabricate stories, or spurious allegations may be made by parents or carers; false and fictitious allegations cause grave injustice; Dr Underwager says that unfounded allegations – the majority – may arise not because children lie but because of interviewers' behaviour. 'He suggested that in the USA some interviewers "lie, threaten, fabricate". The method of assessment contaminates and reduces the reliability of a child's statements, reports Chapter 12.'

The arrangements proposed by the report came to be enshrined in the *Memorandum of Good Practice* published by the Home Office and the Department of Health in 1992. It was pushed through by the Home Office, to the chagrin of many senior practitioners, who participated in a steering group only to find themselves sidelined and yet signed up to a document they did not entirely endorse.

The *Memorandum* follows almost to the letter the procedures proposed by Lord Butler-Sloss. It also incorporates part of Judge Thomas Pigot's report recommending the video recording of children's evidence. But though the 1991 Criminal Justice Act for the first time allowed videoed interviews with a child to be substituted for a child's evidence-in-chief, it still required that children later face cross-examination in person.

According to Professor Graham Davies, an expert on children as witnesses and one of the members of the steering group, distrust of children's testimony influenced the *Memorandum*. The suspicion that children are suggestible 'lies in the origins of the memorandum, in the barristers' concerns about contamination, which is the contemporary version of suggestibility. They are afraid of police officers or social workers putting words into children's mouths.'[8] The *Memorandum* itself issues a stiff warning to its readers: 'The interviews in this memorandum are not and should never be referred to as "therapeutic interviews". Nor should the term "disclosure interview" ever be used to describe them.' Interviews should take place early in an investigation, happen only once, last no more than one hour and be conducted by specially trained social workers and police officers working together.

Did the *Memorandum* facilitate children's stories and their success in the courts? During the nine months after its publication almost 15,000 interviews with child witnesses were videoed. Only 24 per cent were submitted to the Crown Prosecution Service (although this figure masks wide variations between different police forces, ranging from 8 per cent to 64 per cent), and of these very few ever reached a criminal court. On average, the children took 18 minutes to say what they had to say.

Joint interviews became police interviews – in only 2 per cent was there parity between the professionals. The *Memorandum* thus restored police control and social workers felt 'that their expertise and perspective are being devalued and that the investigative process becomes overly prosecution oriented'. With fewer than a quarter of allegations being submitted to the CPS, clearly the protocol pushed children's stories in the wrong direction. Children's cases took an average of 20 weeks to get to court, longer than the overall average.[9]

Since the overwhelming majority of defendants were close to the children – 96 per cent were men, and 82 per cent were related to the children – the protection from direct contact with the defendant afforded by the video link was important. But because the government allowed only evidence-in-chief to be videoed (rather than cross-examination, too) the children's first conversation with the court was cross-examination. Some children have endured days on end behind the video screen. During one organised child abuse trial, which resulted in six adults being gaoled, a child witness for the prosecution was subjected to cross-examination for a week. Observers noticed that the child became increasingly impatient with the interrogators, bewigged men whom the child seemed to suspect of being his father's friends.

The *Memorandum* did not raise the rate of convictions – once late guilty pleas were taken into account, 22 per cent of cases produced a conviction and 27 per cent an acquittal. Child protection professionals within both police and social services were gravely disappointed. What had promised to be a kinder, gentler approach seemed to be just another way of regulating children.

According to Detective Inspector Cath Adams, a veteran of West Yorkshire's child protection service, the *Memorandum* 'only helps those children to whom nothing too serious has happened, who are articulate in the way the jury expects – children who can tell you everything from start to finish'. But that description does not apply to most children who come to the attention of the child protection system. 'Let's say you are involved in an investigation into a family where abuse has gone on for years,' she adds. The *Memorandum* requires an early investigative interview, but 'if you do the interview too early, when the child has not made up its mind about the investigation and is weighing things up, then the child is damned. That is because the child will only tell you what it thinks you need to know to stop the abuse. Remember, you are entering a web of conspiracy and fear. We are asking children to pay a terrible price to give evidence.'[10]

Worse, investigators tended to become focused on procedures and the interview with the child – as if the interview itself were the investigation. In the 1990s it had become commonplace for officers mesmerised by the interview to ignore Home Office circulars on the conduct of investigations – particularly their crisp but critical instruction to collect and preserve evidence.

Two cases in the North-East of England in the 1990s exemplified the effect of Cleveland as the defining moment of the new era:

- In 1992 Toni Dales died. She lived in Middlesbrough and she had not yet reached her fourth birthday. She was brutalised and ultimately killed by Glen McPherson, the man who lived with her mother. Her neighbourhood was a place where men menaced women and children with impunity. An independent report into the circumstances of her death illustrated the state's paralysis when confronted by a deadly man. The independent National Children's Bureau report on her death recorded that no coalition was created with those in the community who were trying to keep the peace while 'bombarded' by men's violence against women and children, and none of the statutory agencies was 'acting on the seriousness of this situation for women and children'. Fatally, the agencies did not share information about McPherson's dangerousness – his civil rights were well respected. He was later jailed.

In what might be regarded as Toni's epitaph, her nursery staff noted that she was solitary, she didn't play, she 'stands alone and cries, puts her face down in her hands and paces backwards and forwards'.

Certainly, multi-disciplinary co-operation improved dramatically in the county after the crisis. But the attack on child protection workers' professional judgement was not immediately redeemed by the enforcement of procedures. It wasn't that the professionals didn't communicate with each other – which had been the Cleveland legend in 1987. They did. They followed the procedures that obliged them to talk to each other about Toni Dales. But did they do any more than that?[11]

- In a now-notorious case involving the alleged abuse of scores, perhaps hundreds, of children in a Tyneside childcare facility, which went to court in the early 1990s police officers abandoned investigations after conducting a videoed interview with a toddler who had just begun to tell the story of what was happening at the nursery. This was the *Memorandum* in practice. This child was vocal, and for many months was giving vivid evidence of people and places to the only detective who seemed interested – his mother. But the beginning and end of that initial investigation was an interview with the accuser, a two-and-a-half-year-old boy. The accused nursery staff, Christopher Lilley and Dawn Reid, denied the allegations.

When more and more children started to tell their stories to their mothers, the statutory services were forced to take them seriously. Although there were clear accounts of the same people and places, according to the police there was no surveillance and the accused's premises were not searched for 14 weeks. Lilley and Reid were acquitted when Mr Justice Holland decreed that he was not prepared to submit these young children to the rigours of the criminal court.[12] In an unprecedented gesture to the children whose courage had exposed an alleged regime of terror and sexual sadism at the nursery and other locales, the local authority made a public announcement: politicians and professionals alike believed the children. In this case it appeared that the obsession with the interviews had obscured the duty to investigate.

The *Memorandum*'s protocol is a model of the template criticised by Sorensen and Snow. Describing the unmasking of abuse as 'a process not an event', they comment that the crisis for children once the story begins to be told is the adult expectation of instant, coherent and detailed accounts.[13] Children typically tell, if they tell at all, with the greatest difficulty.

Commenting on the environment in which child welfare legislation was overhauled in 1991, David Spicer, a barrister, chair of the British Association for the Study and Prevention of Child Abuse and Neglect, and Assistant County Secretary in Nottinghamshire, told an NSPCC national symposium for child protection coordinators in May 1995 that there were among child protection practitioners 'low morale, feelings of vulnerability and isolation, a perceived lack of support and the growing and persistent denial of their expertise and abilities. Commitment is high but cynicism among this group is extensive, particularly with regard to the systems operating and, in particular, the negative impact of the legal processes.' Despite the stated intention to prioritise protection over prosecution 'child protection is increasingly being criminalised', leading to 'gross and inappropriate misapplication of resources'.

The approach to interviewing children 'owes little to the collective wisdom of child-centred professionals and more to the application of judge-made rules and rigid/inflexible principles of evidence'. Spicer was particularly alarmed by the domination of the criminal courts' standards of proof – beyond reasonable doubt – in civil proceedings where, hitherto, all concerned parties had been able to air their concerns and the civil standard – balance of probabilities – had determined the child's entitlement to protection, though not, of course, the culpability of the alleged perpetrator. 'Proceedings are now far more adversarial than those conducted under the previous legislation and involve more personnel, whose own interest lies in the exaggeration of contentious issues.' According to Spicer, the stiffening of standards of proof in civil proceedings 'ensures that the more serious the concerns, the more vulnerable the child, the more difficult it is to provide protection for that child'. This encouraged 'in those responsible for providing a caring and safe environment for a child an interest in persistent denial'.

Spicer's concern that it was becoming ever more difficult to provide protection for children being oppressed physically, sexually and emotionally, coincided with a new approach from the Department of Health promoting a shift away from 'child protection' towards 'family support'.

'Those engaged in the child protection system, and particularly social workers, have lost their way,' said Wendy Rose, the Department of Health's Assistant Chief Inspector, when in 1995 she announced the new approach, which was based on research commissioned in the aftermath of Cleveland. A strong intimation of the tone of the new thinking was 'Parental Perspectives in Cases of Suspected Child Abuse' by Hedy Cleaver and Pam Freeman, who sneered that the 'legacy of investigations' – broken marriages, children in care – so 'violating to families' were 'high prices to pay for a bruise or children witnessing a spicy video'.[14]

Summarising the research, Michael Little, deputy director of the Dartington Social Research Unit acknowledged in seminars conducted throughout Britain that more abuse was being uncovered and that the 'sheer weight of referrals coming into the system' meant that the 'threshold for intervention is, conversely, moving upwards'.[15]

Little appealed not for reform and re-investment in this exhausted system, but for re-alignment of its priorities away from investigation. This was proposed in the context of the pauperisation of large numbers of people, polarisation of classes at a greater rate than anywhere else in Europe, the demonisation of children in the 1990s and the emergence of a new political subject – the father as victim, supported by the only mass movement mobilised by fathers: against the Child Support Agency.

Wendy Rose, like Michael Little, argued that child protection priorities after Cleveland had to be 'balanced against the considerable public concern that mistakes had been made'. The Department of Health seemed to be alluding to parents, not children. Children in Britain did not and do not get the support services they deserve. The dominant ideology of the medical establishment remained

Freudian and therefore, in the main, uninformed by the traumatic stress of sexual abuse.

'When he put it in I thought I was going to die. I know what that feels like, to die. I'll never forget it,' said a ten-year-old child abused by her grandfather in the 1990s. We now know that for many children staying alive feels too hard and they, like this child, have to decide, every day, to live. Or die. And she thinks she knows what that feels like.

Wendy Rose's concern was that 'parents and carers felt threatened' and the child protection process had been dominated by a 'forensic approach'. That, however, was the monster the government itself had created. The adversarial atmosphere and the criminalised culture of child protection were a direct effect of the government's denigration of welfare professionals and its attempts to 'balance' irreconcilable interests. Far from returning to a child-centred ethic, the government proposed to appease affronted adults by applying a 'lighter touch'.

Here was history repeating itself, this time not as farce but as tragedy again.

Notes

1 Roland Summit, 'The Centrality of Victimization', in *Psychiatric Clinics of North America*, Vol. 12, No. 2, June 1989.

2 The Rt Hon Lord Justice Butler-Sloss, 'The Cleveland Enquiry', in the *Medico-Legal Journal*, Vol. 57, No. 3, 1989.

3 Roland Summit, 'The Child Sexual Abuse Accommodation Syndrome', in *Child Abuse and Neglect*, Vol. 17, pp.177–93, 1983.

4 Anna Salter, *Accuracy of Expert Testimony in Child Sexual Abuse Cases. A Case Study of Ralph Underwager and Hollida Wakefield.*

5 Roland Summit, 'The Centrality of Victimization', *ibid*.

6 Teena Sorensen and Barbara Snow, 'How Children Tell: The Process of Disclosure in Child Sexual Abuse', in *Child Welfare*, Vol. 70, No. 1, Jan–Feb 1991.

7 Judith Dawson Jones, in a paper presented to a child protection conference at Birkbeck College, London, June 1994.

8 Interview with Beatrix Campbell, The *Independent*, 20 October 1993.

9 Graham Davies, Clare Wilson, Rebecca Mitchell and John Milsom, *Videotaping Children's Evidence*, Leicester University, 1995.

10 Interview with Beatrix Campbell, The *Independent*, 20 October 1993.

11 *Investigation into Inter-Agency Practice Following the Cleveland Area Child Protection Committee's Report Concerning the Death of Toni Dales*, National Children's Bureau, London, March 1993.

12 Beatrix Campbell, 'We All Fall Down', The *Guardian*, 17 August 1994.

13 Teena Sorensen and Barbara Snow, 'How Children Tell: The Process of Disclosure of Sexual Abuse', in *Child Welfare*, Vol. 70, No. 1, Jan–Feb 1991.

14 Hedy Cleaver and Pam Freeman, *Parental Perspectives in Cases of Suspected Child Abuse*, HMSO, 1995.

15 *Child Protection: messages from research* by Dartington Social Research Unit, HMSO, 1995.